Testimonies of Discipleship:

Stories from the Local Church

By
Mark Barbee

© 2016

Dear Mandy + Dave,
Thanks for being our dear friends
over several years. Hope this is inspiring
to you. God Bless —

Mark

Contents

Prelude

My life has been filled with music, so I begin this story with a musical term. There have been many "movements", blessings and opportunities. My life has been enriched by many people. The book began with "Pauls and Timothies" as a working title and that still describes the theme pretty well. However, lest you think these stories are only about men, there are also many women in these pages that have influenced me and hopefully gained some encouragement from me. We have had a number of ladies teach and disciple others through the years.

The Bible speaks about the power of testimony and I hope these stories will be encouraging to you. *"They overcame him (the accuser) by the blood of the lamb and by the word of their testimony."*[1] There are also many other significant people from my years in ministry, but no book can name everyone. I have tried to use testimonies that are varied and fun to read about. Please don't feel neglected if you do not find your name somewhere. These God stories will help you get a rough idea of the story of Fairfield Christian Church over the last three decades through the eyes of disciples and leaders.

The book is autobiographical to the extent that it illustrates discipleship woven through the chapters of my life. Perhaps these stories will remind you to appreciate those who have discipled you. Of course I

---

[1] Revelation 12:11

hope that it will also spur you to consider discipling or continuing to disciple others. I hope you appreciate my sense of humor as we move through these pages together. Discipleship is not all serious!

There are favorite Scriptures and songs through the pages of this book. I could not possibly say which ones are most important to me. These verses and lyrics have all strengthened me over the years, along with many, many others.

(Unless otherwise noted, quotations are from the NIV Bible.)

I am grateful to the faithful people and leaders of Fairfield Christian Church for serving as a laboratory for discipleship for me and others over more than thirty years. The ministry of this church goes far beyond what you see at any given moment. The best days of this church are yet to come.

I dedicate this book to my grandchildren, and hope that it will be a blessing to each of them as they are old enough to read and understand it: Aaron, Evan, Abbie, Michael, and Claire.

"To God be the glory, great things He has done."

Mark Barbee, 2016

Chapter One

The main theme of this story is the discipleship I have observed and experienced. I must give credit for those who mentored and shaped me in my early years. I am grateful for a number of people who discipled me. So before I share the many stories that are part of Fairfield Church, I want to share part of my story with you.

What is discipleship? Though I have seen many definitions over the years, I believe in a very simple one: spending a period of time with someone that allows God to encourage them in spiritual growth! It doesn't have to be a formal meeting, though it can be. The length of time of these relationships has varied greatly for me, from a few months to a few years. Much of my discipling experience has been informal; in homes, restaurants and music rehearsals. Some has certainly been in classrooms. A lot of it has been in hospitals. With Jesus, discipleship involved learning, following and serving.

This is also a book about testimonies of which I have been a small part. There are over thirty of these faith stories in this collection. It is a blessing to be used by God, in whatever small way, to encourage others. Out of these relationships have also come some principles that I have included. Moreover, this is a story of the local church and how it works to disciple people. Regarding the local church, I recently read a beautiful tribute from Bill Hybels:

The local church is the hope of the world....

There is nothing like the local church when it's working right. Its beauty is indescribable. Its power is breathtaking. Its potential is unlimited. It comforts the grieving and heals the broken in the context of community. It builds bridges to seekers and offers truth to the confused. It provides resources for those in need and opens its arms to the forgotten, the downtrodden, the disillusioned.[2]

There are other stories that could be included in this book, but these are the ones the Spirit has brought to mind. Don't expect a lot of high profile, famous people in these pages. But the goal is show how God works in ordinary people like you and me! Let me start with my testimony. I'm not so much speaking of my earthly heritage, as in ancestry, but of my spiritual heritage. Mine is a testimony of God's faithfulness and how my life has been blessed by the church. The stories and testimonies from Fairfield Church begin in Chapter Two. But first a little background.

My Early Years

My father Frank lived only two years after I was born. But I had his parents in my life for eleven years. I knew that they prayed for me, their only grandchild. My father was a WW II veteran and sometime student at Ohio State. He went to Officer Candidate School and

---

[2] Bill Hybels, *Courageous Leadership,* Zondervan, 2002, pg.15, 23.

became a First Lieutenant in the Army, serving in Italy. He was an Episcopalian and I still have his study Bible.

My mother Frances grew up in a solid Christian family. Her dad taught adults in Sunday school. Grandma played the organ most Sundays. Mom's uncles were teachers and elders in churches. After my dad died, she took me to the independent Christian church in the south end of Columbus. That church on Southwood Avenue shaped my early years. My mom loved music and was a natural alto. She was in the choir every Sunday and I tried to behave myself on the third pew while she was in the choir loft. By the way, our church had keyboards and I was asked to play the trumpet a few times during my Junior and Senior High school years.[3] I was also in my first play, preached my first sermon and sang my first solo at Southwood.

In my early years, my (maternal) Grandpa Fulwider was my hero and friend. He loved the Bible, history, and teaching industrial arts. He taught Adult Sunday School for many years in his little Methodist Church. I learned to use tools from him. I obviously got some of my love of the Bible and history from him. I must have gotten some of his genes because I still like to do an occasional project around the house. Some of his personality surely passed through my mother to me. My Grandma had the musical gift, playing organ or piano most every Sunday in church.

---

[3] While I liked popular music, my idols were trumpet players like Al Hirt, Herb Alpert and Doc Severinsen. Later, Chicago was my favorite group.

Instilling the Word

Love the Lord your God with all your heart, and with all your soul and with all your strength. These commandments that I give you today are to be upon your hearts. Impress them on your children... Deuteronomy 6:5

I was blessed to hear God's word through many Sunday school teachers and our pastor. We also had revivals every year with guest preachers. My first Bible was a gift from the church. It was the King James Version and somewhat difficult, but I learned a lot from it.

I had many good public school teachers. Don't tell anyone, but I learned the Ten Commandments from my fifth grade teacher. We also recited the Lord's Prayer and the Bill of Rights. I'm sure it warped me! A couple years later it was Nov. 22, 1963. My Junior High principal announced on the PA that the president had been shot in Dallas. He said "I don't care what the Supreme Court said, we're going to stop and pray." Hmmm. Food for thought: prayer in schools outlawed, president assassinated, Viet Nam War starts... Just a coincidence? Or did we forsake God's wisdom and protection?

My home pastor came when I was seven and I soon experienced a little red headed tornado, the Preacher's Kid. Mark Wesner eventually became my friend, but at first all he did was beat on my arm. He was hyper. I must have been a calming influence on him because his mother liked me. As we grew older, she also directed our teen choir. Later Mark W. and I managed to break a few church windows together with balls and bikes. We played church basketball and softball together. We had great laughs reading Mad Magazine together. We later learned to play 12 string guitars independently from one another, about the same time, in different colleges! We played at campfires together at church camp a few of those summers. Mark also went on to spend his life in ministry. We have done several retreats together and are still friends.

My Salvation

From the time I was ten years old I began to think about accepting Jesus and being baptized. I was finally ready to talk with our pastor, Ellis Wesner, about this decision. He came to the house with a deacon named Vern and shared Scriptures with me. Some of them I had already learned at Sunday school, church and camp. (I realize now that Ellis was discipling that deacon.) I still remember the Sunday after I had turned eleven, getting baptized at the invitation time. I stood in the baptistery and repeated the good confession, "Jesus is the Christ, the Son of the living God, and I've accepted him as my Lord and Savior". Ellis would always say "dead unto sin, and alive unto Christ" during the baptism.

My Mentors

Ellis Wesner, became my mentor: especially when, at age 14, I began to work on the God and Country Award in Scouting. That required me to work with him for over a year. He had me memorize some longer passages like John 1: 1-14. He had me read Through the Bible that year. This set up a discipling experience aimed at receiving an award after a year. But it became much more than that. That experience has paid dividends throughout my life. Ellis became my model of what a pastor should be. At the end of that period, when I was 15, I felt called to go into ministry.

During that season I sat under the teaching of an elder named Art Scott, a retired engineer. I loved the way he analyzed the Bible and made it understandable. I was about the only teenager in Art's class while Mom was in choir practice. (I had graduated to class eventually after spending some early years crawling under pews during Mom's choir time.) Also around that time we attended a Billy Graham Crusade in Columbus.

Later I would realize that these men were discipling me. I will always think it Providential that Ellis and his family were with us those ten years until I was seventeen. Vern Banker worked with our youth group and taught me II Peter 3:18- "but grow in grace and in the knowledge of our Lord and Savior Jesus Christ." Eleanor and John Tope were our youth sponsors and took some of us to visit Bible colleges in Kentucky and Cincinnati.

Summers at Round Lake Christian camp gave me hope that there were other cute Christian girls out there besides the handful in our youth group. Oh yeah, we also learned some Bible stuff. Seriously, I memorized many Bible verses during those weeks. In high school, a local youth leader named Hugh Snepp (Hugh was a public school teacher and a pastor) must have seen something in me and asked me to be an officer in Teens for Christ.

Before I leave this heritage section, I must mention my Uncles and Aunts. My Uncle Harold took me under his wing, along with his own four kids. Harold James had a tire business in which I later worked and got my hands dirty each summer. Harold had survived being wounded in the Battle of the Bulge to come home and marry my Aunt Betty.[4] Harold guided me through seasons of life and was a father to me. He was also active in church along with Aunt Betty. She was the one who helped me pass my driving test. My uncle was part of my ordination service, when I was set apart for the ministry.

Uncle Bill, my mother's brother, was a journalist and lover of classical music. On the other hand, his wife Pat loved the Beatles and that's the album I would

---

[4] Their four kids are like brothers and sisters. My cousin Craig and I did Scouting trips together, including a 110 mile hike in Michigan and a trip to Philmont in New Mexico. We both made Eagle our senior year.

listen to when I visited them. They helped keep me open to the arts. They were proud of me when I played "The Music Man" my senior year at South High School.[5] So, in spite of being from a relatively modest, single parent home in the south end, I was blessed in many ways.

By the way, my high school band director influenced me in two ways my senior year. Syd Townsend was an alumnus of the Ohio State Marching Band and encouraged me to try out. Stranger than that, however, was the day he asked me to try out for the lead in "The Music Man". He had never seen me sing or act, but for some reason he encouraged me that way. **God had a plan.** I memorized the "Trouble" monologue for tryouts and got the part. I enjoyed singing, acting and being in front of people. Our vocal teacher, Jim Gallagher, gave me some free vocal tips.[6] That these two men's years at South High coincided with mine is still a wonder to me.

If you think about it, maybe you can identify the discipling principle at work through various people in your early years.

---

[5] My four younger cousins came with them. David Fulwider, the oldest, was about ten at the time and still remembers it!

[6] The next year, Syd moved on to the Westerville School system. Years later, Dr. Gallagher was teaching at Ohio State and my daughter Rachel was in one of his vocal groups.

Discipleship Defined

Discipleship discussions usually start with Jesus and the Twelve Disciples. That's how I started my thesis on discipling early in my ministry. We talked then of how discipleship involves learning, following and serving the Master. Those elements still apply. But in practice I've found the discipling process to be quite different from the ideal.

One of the biggest differences in Jesus' process was the time element. Almost no one has the luxury (or radical commitment) to spend the majority of their time with someone for three years. So everything we do is an adaptation. Perhaps, if we're blessed, it could be once a week for three years. Often, it's less than that in actual personal time spent. Rarely is it more, although experiencing the same teaching and worship in groups is certainly part of the process. Jesus' disciples likely memorized his main speeches and teachings.

Usually, discipleship is some combination—sitting under the same teaching for an hour a week, mixed with personal times that are usually less frequent than that. The personal times vary from one time to another and one disciple to another—from study or visitation together, to recreation. So in this collection I have written some inspiring testimonies of my times with a wide variety of individuals and circumstances, and the way God has used the Body of Christ in a variety of ways to minister to them.

Some of the other discipling stories in Scripture get a little closer to our experiences. Paul's relationship with Timothy is a popular example. And we can draw upon Paul's letters to Timothy to look more closely at that. In that case, Paul's instruction trained Timothy to be a church leader, but much of his instruction is useful to all of us. Paul describes discipleship very succinctly in II Tim. 2: 2:

> *And the things you have heard me say in the presence of many witnesses entrust to reliable men who will also be qualified to teach others.*

I've looked at that verse from both sides now and I have some wonderful stories of how it has worked in my life and relationships. The vast majority of my time has been spent with men, but I mention how women have been discipled in the life of the church as well. The stories involve many wives and husbands and how God united them spiritually and through strengthening their marriage.

Are there areas in which you've been discipling someone without realizing it?

Scarlet and Gray Years

I decided to go to Ohio State because it was close, inexpensive, and I wanted to be in the marching band. I figured I could get a broad education and then go to Bible College and pursue the ministry. My favorite elder, Art, was worried, though. He was afraid I would go to the university and lose my faith. I figured that my faith needed to be stronger than that and I took it as a challenge. I never heard any information (or theories) that seriously challenged my faith. And I was always able to find good conservative writers and teachers and so learn from the skeptical challenges. More about that in a moment.

God blessed me in many ways in those years. I majored in secondary education, concentrating in history. My first week on campus was tryouts week for the Ohio State University Marching Band. I made the band and had great experiences in the next four years, including two Rose Bowl trips and a presidential inaugural. My second year I switched to flugelhorn, a mellower sounding version of the trumpet. I still get to see most of my band friends at alumni band football games and other events. If you are a Buckeye fan, then you know the thrill of the Ramp Entrance and the Script Ohio. It's definitely an adrenaline rush to march on that field with around a hundred thousand watching. (Believe it or not, in the old days, they actually televised part of the half time show!)

One challenge for me was a Bible as Literature course. In many colleges, such courses sounded innocent, but were used to undermine basic faith in the Bible. The text and professor followed some simple rules: the supernatural and predictive prophecy are rejected *a priori.*[7] We used a "study Bible" that was the most liberal at that time. *The Dartmouth Bible* was filled

---

[7] Based on presupposed theory rather than on observation.

with liberal theories about the Old Testament in particular: the Pentateuch was not written by Moses; Isaiah was not written by Isaiah; you get the picture. A small group of us pointed out this bias in class, but the professor was not sympathetic.

I was able to find great Old Testament scholars such as E. J. Young that had already answered the liberal objections. Unfortunately, most students in those classes were more likely to accept the undermining of Scripture as part of their coming of age. **I still believe that every church needs to be intentional about preparing high school kids for the challenge of secular philosophies—they need apologetics!**

But my spiritual development accelerated at Ohio State, thanks to student Christian organizations like Student Christian Foundation and Campus Crusade. I taught Bible studies for the SCF and learned to play guitar (it's a little difficult to play trumpet and sing at the same time!) Of course it was the season to learn guitar! It was also an opportunity to hear Josh McDowell for the first time. He traveled for Campus Crusade at the time. He spoke in the student union on two exciting topics- Bible prophecy and "maximum sex" (within marriage). Both topics drew a pretty good crowd. Later he came out with his great work *Evidence That Demands a Verdict.*

Some friends and I went to Dallas in 1972 for a huge student event called Explo 72. There we were introduced to contemporary Christian music, along with nearly 100,000 young people. Rock and roll for Jesus! Larry Norman sang, "Why should the devil have all the good music?" One of Larry's most enduring songs was a simple folk tune called "I Wish We'd All Been Ready". Andrae Crouch and Love Song were two of the big groups at Explo.

We also talked a lot about witnessing and baptized some kids in a swimming pool. In the process I learned a valuable lesson about letting the Bible speak. A couple friends wanted to debate baptism and I simply said, "let's look at some Scriptures right now." Within a few minutes of looking in the book of Acts, they were ready to jump in the pool. We loved the music, the preaching and filling the Cotton Bowl every night. We liked having our "foot on the rock and our name on the roll". Exciting times!

Explo 72 closed with a candle-lighting and commissioning service led by Billy Graham. I had nearly forgotten about that part until recently a movie referenced it! The movie *Woodlawn* is the true story about a football team and chaplain in Birmingham at the height of the Jesus Movement. The movie is about the power of Jesus' love to change a community struggling with segregation. The chaplain had been motivated by the candle lighting at Explo '72!

By the time I graduated from Ohio State, I had met my wife and we formed a band. We sang and played together and were joined by a couple guitar players, a keyboard player, and my cousin on the drums. As I started to attend Cincinnati Bible Seminary part time, **we also began an inner city street ministry called His Place.** We hoped to disciple inner city kids. But we probably did more discipling with our volunteer counselors and Christian band members than we were able to do with street kids.

The Jesus Movement

While not exactly a "discipling" event, the Jesus Movement influenced us greatly. In late 1972 there was an explosion among youth around our country. Many young people were by this time disillusioned by the "free love" movement and the false promises of the Woodstock generation. They were turning to Christ. Young pastors were reaching out to "long hairs" and letting down their hair (even though some were half bald). Like many cultural events, the movement gained momentum in Southern California through concerts and mass baptisms in the ocean. "Jesus Music" was a big part of the movement and soon Christian radio was picking up on contemporary music, and not just Gospel music. Even the Doobie Brothers sang "Jesus Is Just Alright With Me".

Though many churches were uptight and hesitant to depart from their liturgy and traditions, many others threw open their doors and morphed into churches that could attract all kinds of young people. Pastors like Chuck Smith and Jack Hayford reached out in love to the "Jesus Generation".

Time Magazine featured "the Jesus Movement" on its cover and tried to understand it. I was taking a sociology class that winter and wrote a paper on the Jesus Movement. Of course it was close to my heart and I felt part of it. The professor was impressed and thought I should change my major from history to sociology. Instead, I graduated, formed a band and started in an inner city "street ministry" later that year. We worked out of a store front with volunteer "counselors". My job was to recruit and train counselors from churches. **That turned out to be another form of discipleship for believers who were learning some basic evangelism skills.**

Forty Years Later

We could use another Jesus Movement today. It left young people like myself inspired, in both music and ministry. It raised up a new generation of church leaders and new brotherhoods of churches. It brought new music into the church at large and led to a fresh movement of worship. At times it coincided with the charismatic movement of the seventies. People were having fresh experiences with the Holy Spirit.

As with every revival, not everyone sustains those experiences. But most of the fruit has been absorbed into the church at large and has changed the church at the same time. In those days, I never thought praise bands would be a regular part of the weekly church format. Fresh music has been a fresh vehicle for the gospel. One of the first songs I ever wrote was from Psalm 150:

Praise the Lord, Praise ye the Lord

Praise God in his sanctuary

Praise him in the firmament; praise him for his excellent greatness.

Praise him with trumpet sound; praise him with harp and lyre

Praise him with timbrel and dance

Praise him with the loud cymbals, praise him with resounding cymbals.

Praise him with strings and pipe.

Let everything that has breath, praise the Lord.[8]

We took those words literally, and used everything that makes a sound in praise to the Lord. Our band used all our instruments on that song, making sure the trumpet, lead guitar and drums all had solos. We liked the loud part, of course, in our concerts.

Full Circle

Last summer I had the privilege (along with our local ministers group) of hosting one of the greatest guitarists of all time in our town. His name? Phil Keaggy. In 1970 he had an up and coming rock band

---

[8] Lyrics adapted from "Psalm 150" by M. Barbee and B. Houchins.

called Glass Harp in the Youngstown area. A couple years later he was saved and dedicated his music to the Lord. I had met him briefly in the late seventies. By then he had done several Christian albums and fronted various bands. He could play any guitar and any style. He wrote a song called "Full Circle" which I have always loved, talking about his journey with the Lord. After picking up Phil and his wife up at the airport, we immediately reminisced about life over the last few decades. It helps being the same age! I told Phil and his wife, Bernadette, how we appreciated their faithfulness over all these years. It felt like a "full circle" event for me. Now, back to the seventies.

Our band played a lot of concerts during those years, from coffee houses to churches, and recorded an album (on vinyl, of course). We also attended a lot of concerts with up and coming contemporary Christian artists. Andrae Crouch, Love Song, Second Chapter of Acts, Keith Green and Phil Keaggy were among our favorite groups and artists.

During those years, I was challenged to believe all of God's Word and not just what I had grown up with. We learned some things about grace, worship and the Holy Spirit that have stayed with me for forty years now. We had a son, Matt, and daughter, Rachel, during those years. They were a great joy to me.

Chapter Two

The God Squad- Steve

I just got a letter from a longtime friend and my first "Timothy". That's what we call someone we have helped disciple who goes on into ministry. Steve Elkins came into our youth group right after I returned from Explo 72. I was working at my home church as summer youth minister. He was fourteen, I was twenty-one. He was an enthusiastic young protégé. Today we would call him a "mini me". He learned to play the 12 string so we could lead worship together. He brought other kids in and we had a great team that summer and the following one. We called the group, the God Squad. (Some older readers might remember the TV show called Mod Squad.)

I was able to keep track of Steve as I graduated from college and began the street ministry. Steve was in the audience when our Christian band played. Later he went on to Bible Seminary and became a pastor. Because my graduate studies were on hold a few years, he actually finished at Cincinnati before I did! He has served as both a lead pastor and associate pastor and is still serving today. Here is a principle for youth workers: **The time you invest in youth ministry will bear fruit for decades to come!**

This season in my life would not have been possible without the care of my pastor and mentor Carl Pruitt. Carl came to our church after Ellis and began preaching for what would be my college years. Thanks to him, I was hired as summer youth minister and able to start the God Squad. Carl later taught psychology and counseling in Christian college. But for a time, he preached and led us and encouraged my ministry. I learned some good things about hospital visitation from him.

Carl led the committee from my home church that ordained me into Christian ministry in June of 1975. I was blessed to have Carl, some local church elders, and some of my uncles who were elders, all participate in the laying on of hands that launched me into ministry just forty years ago.[9]

We were a New Testament Church. We believed in the church as revealed in the book of Acts. We are in the New Covenant. But Carl wanted to do a series on the Old Testament, where he still made New Testament applications to Christ and the Christian life. I will always appreciate Carl's concern for me and my ministry. One of my favorite sayings is: **The Old Testament contains the New concealed: the New Testament contains the Old revealed**.

Academically speaking, I was blessed by good professors at Cincinnati during those years, including Dr. Jack Cottrell and Dr. Lewis Foster.

---

[9] One of those elders was Mark Ebersole, who later influenced me to move to Lancaster and be part of a church led by Frank Dawson.

From Andrae' Crouch to the Imperials

This lyric from Andrae's song *My Tribute* became a life theme for me:

> *How can I say thanks, for the things you have done for me?*
>
> *Things so undeserved, yet you give to prove your love for me.*
>
> *The voices of a million angels could not express my gratitude.*
>
> *All that I am and ever hope to be, I owe it all to you.*
>
> *To God be the glory, to God be the glory*
>
> *To God be the glory for the things He has done.*
>
> *By his blood He has saved me, by his power He has raised me*
>
> *To God be the glory for the things He has done.*
>
> *Just let me live my life and let it be pleasing Lord to Thee*
>
> *And should I gain any praise, let it go to Calvary!*[10]

Andrae' Crouch and the Disciples was a young black gospel group from Los Angeles. Andrae' brought a new style of music that today would be called urban, rhythm and blues and choral all at the same time. He

---

[10] My Tribute by Andrae' Crouch

always featured at least four singers, two girls and two guys. He played the piano like I had never seen before. We first heard them at Explo 72. In the next year, he exploded onto the Christian music scene and was playing concerts and festivals all over the United States. In the next twenty years he would play in over forty countries. Andrae's message was always the gospel! The lyrics were simple, but the music was contemporary, bordering on jazz. Black choirs loved it. White audiences loved it. He bridged the racial gap in the church. Something of his spirit infected me. It's always helped me sing with a little more "soul". Our band did a lot of his music. I had grown up in a racially balanced high school (Columbus South) and enjoyed most of the "soul" music of that time (now called R&B.) He eventually performed at Billy Graham crusades and on the Gaither Homecoming series.

What I realize now is that Andrae' was always a discipler. He discipled members of his group who came and went over the years. He impacted Christian music for a generation and wrote several classics. He discipled many of us from a distance. In January (2015), Andrae' passed on to the Glory that he had sung about for over fifty years. Our local churches did a special tribute night with some of his great songs, including "My Tribute".

I was not into southern gospel music, except for a crossover group named the Imperials. Yes, they were a four part male quartet, but they did increasingly contemporary styles of music. They featured the first black singer in an otherwise white group.[11] People today cannot fully grasp what that did for the church in positive ways. The church has made a lot of progress in breaking down racial barriers, but there is much more needed. Armond, Terry, Sherman and Jim are still some of my favorite singers ever.[12] Later, they added Russ Taff for some of their hits in the 80's.[13]

Unexpecteds

After five years, the inner city street ministry faded out and I was called by the Columbus Public Schools to teach in Middle School. (I had been on their substitute teacher list.) It seemed like good tent-making for a time. After all, the Apostle Paul made tents during and between ministry times. What I thought would be a year turned into five. I had always wanted a broad background before settling into ministry and God used this period to give me background in the secular work world. I still have a special place in my heart for teachers! Today our two daughters work in public schools.

After three years, I was laid off in a year of massive school layoffs. Meanwhile, my wife worked as a pediatric physical therapist. I became a daily substitute teacher, which is no picnic. But it did allow me to reenroll in my Masters' Program at Cincinnati Bible Seminary (today Cincinnati Christian University).

---

[11] Sherman Andrus

[12] Armond Morales, Terry Blackwood, Sherman Andrus, Jim Murray

[13] Russ was featured on "Praise the Lord" and "Trumpet of Jesus".

I wrote my thesis on "Discipling in the Local Congregation".

Meanwhile we had some unexpected experiences with a local church. They believed in discipleship and worship, which we liked. We even moved from Columbus to Lancaster to be part of this church and community. I liked their openness to the Holy Spirit, but I also found that their approach was unpredictable. I hoped for a while that God might open doors for me there for full time ministry. It was not to be. Would I get to minister again and how long would it take? The Lord gave me a song at that time:

Doors close and I know it's God,

But somehow there's a hurt in my heart.

When visions crumble, when prospects fade,

He's made a change in the plans I've made

Which direction should I go?

This way or that, I go to the Lord

My situation is in his plan,

It's far greater than the mind of man.[14]

---

[14] "Renewing the Vision" by M. Barbee

The School of the Holy Spirit

So I say to you: Ask and it will be given to you; seek and you will find;

Knock and the door will be opened to you...

If you then, though you are evil, know how to give good gifts to your children,

How much more will your Father in heaven give the Holy Spirit

To those who ask him! Lk. 11: 9-11

Back in the Apollo space program days, when American astronauts were going to the moon, there was a term called Trans Lunar Injection. This was the point at which the rocket fired to boost the Apollo capsule out of earth's orbit and into the trajectory to the moon. It took extra energy to loose them from earth's gravity.

That reminds me of the power of the Holy Spirit when we seek his energy to loose us from the everyday gravity of life and set us on a higher path. Jesus said we could ask for this power! Yet many people never do. It takes a certain amount of emptying of ourselves in order to let the Spirit fill us. I've had a few of those experiences in my life. One was while I was in college.

I had been trying to figure out logically what certain Bible verses meant. I met some fellow believers who, despite their education and intelligence, knew that logic could only go so far. **So I took a step of faith, a step of surrender, and asked the Lord to fill me anew with His Holy Spirit.** There was a fresh joy in my life. It was not a time of desperation, only a desire to go deeper with the Lord.

Over the next few months my prayer life was blessed, my worship life was blessed, and I began teaching Bible classes in my college group. I have had other "fillings" with the Spirit since that time that have led to the inspiration to write songs, sermons, an Easter drama and eventually several books. The Holy Spirit gives us all kinds of giftings—not just the ones listed in Paul's letters.

I am neither a "Cessasionist"[15] nor a "Sensationalist". We should not put God in a box, saying that He will not do the things that were done in the early church, nor expect Him to do everything in us that He did in the Apostles. Truth is somewhere in between. That's why we have to empty ourselves in order to let Him work.

I have prayed for many sick people over my years of ministry. Some have been healed, some have not. It is part of the mystery of God and His will as to why this is so. But we try to empathize with those folks and share hope from God's Word. Suffice it to say that God has used us to bless people. We go in faith and leave the results to Him. **It's up to the God of our faith, not the amount of our faith.**

---

[15] A Cessationist believes that certain gifts of the Holy Spirit were only given in the first century. This is a misinterpretation of a few verses of Scripture.

I am thankful that over the years we have encouraged our elders to pray for the sick when requested, according to James 5:14. It is usually some combination of elders and pastors that have prayed in hospital rooms, homes, prayer rooms and you name it. Since all of us are ordained shepherds, we do not make an issue of how many are "elders" or "pastors", or other brethren that want to pray with us.[16] One thing that is always present in these prayers is the love of God flowing through us to His people.

> *Is any of you sick? He should call the elders of the church to pray over him and anoint him with oil in the name of the Lord. And the prayer offered in faith will make the sick person well; the Lord will raise him up. If he has sinned, he will be forgiven. Therefore confess your sins to each other and pray for each other so that you may be healed. The prayer of a righteous man is powerful and effective. James 5: 14-16*

For the last fifteen years I have taken men with me on hospital and nursing home visits. Some have been elders, others not. But each one has helped me tremendously in a difficult ministry. It is not only difficult in the wide variety of situations that you walk into, but also in the sense of being a marathon over many years. Some situations are minor, some are death bed experiences.

---

[16] Pastors are paid elders according to I Tim. 5: 17. Ordination is the biblical practice of laying on hands to set apart for ministry.

Hundreds of people that we have prayed for have come and gone from our church. Sometimes it does feel like work, but it is always better to have another man of faith with me. Many times we drive thirty or forty minutes to some of the hospitals we cover. As the Proverb says, "two are better than one". I suspect it is as much of a blessing to these men to pray and be used by God as it is a blessing to me. Some of their testimonies will appear in the coming pages.

But these years of ministry might not have happened if not for a few visionary men thirty years ago.

Invited to a Party and the Host Left

1983 was filled with both hope and disappointment for me. I tried to hold on to the lyrics of a song by Phil Keaggy; "disappointment, His appointment". This is what happened. A local minister invited me to meet with him and share my testimony. He called me a few weeks later and said he thought he had a position he wanted me to consider. He wanted a part time worship leader and associate for adults.

I met with some elders and found them good agreeable men. **Howard had discipled them well in the ten years he had been at Fairfield Church.** Ken, Steve, Larry, and Richard were a great bunch: an engineer, doctor, accountant and chemistry teacher.[17] Things seemed to be favorable and my position was

---

[17] Ken Brooks, Dr. Steve Miller, Larry Cox, Richard Smith.

approved. Jeff Connar was the youth pastor and really encouraged me in this process.

But then I didn't hear anything for a few weeks. What was going on? I finally called Howard[18], only to learn that he had taken a position at a church in Indiana. I was disappointed. It was like a carrot had been held out and then removed. The leaders didn't want to add a new position until they found a new preaching minister. That was understandable, but still difficult.

On the other hand, they did ask us to come and do music for a series of meetings that fall. We were happy to do so but didn't understand what God was doing. However it was a great week of meetings. Let me digress for a moment.

Discipled in the Creation Science Movement

The heavens declare the glory of God; the skies proclaim the work of his hands. Day after day they pour forth speech; night after night they display knowledge. There is no speech or language where their voice is not heard. Ps. 19: 1-3

While a student at the Ohio State University, I took geology and anthropology classes, enough to see that there were a lot of holes in evolution. The most zealous professors were at times illogical and a little nutty. I began to see that for them this was a religion. But I also learned some tools for evaluating science

---

[18] Howard Brammer went to Traders Point Christian Church and served many years.

and the difference between hard science and theoretical science. That distinction has been all but lost in the last few decades. Until 1983 I was somewhere between being a Creationist and wondering if God could have used some evolution.

A seminar in 1983 caused me to reject Darwinian evolution entirely for lack of evidence. (We understand that microevolution, or change within species, does occur.) A more scientific explanation of creation, the flood of Noah and biological theories helped me realize that evolution was even weaker than I had thought. The presenter was a NASA scientist. He gave a day's worth of information and could have filled several days. His name was Walter Brown. **He exposed evolution's dirty little secret: there is circular reasoning between the time scales of the geologists and paleontologists!** "This rock is that old because of the fossils in it; this fossil is that old because it's found in that layer!"

The flood of Noah is a <u>better</u> explanation for the fossil/geologic record than evolution. I also became aware of the Institute for Creation Research out of California. I realized that many PhD's had joined the organization, including biologists and physicists. Dr. Henry Morris and Dr. Dwayne Gish enjoyed touring campuses and debating evolution with whoever would face them. Later the work of Ken Ham and Answers in Genesis inspired many of our congregation when we had him speak here in the year 2,000.

The age of the universe is still a big debate. We must remember that it, too, is based on assumptions about the age of elements, rate of radioactive decay, starlight, etc. It is a mystery. I think that someday the theory of relativity will help us understand the apparent age of the universe and the recent age of the earth. (It is obvious that many evidences for a young earth have been suppressed by evolutionary theory.) Biological evolution from one species to another is impossible because there have been no missing links discovered in a hundred and fifty years of searching. If evolution were true there would be thousands.

One day, I believe we will see that evolution and global warming are two of the greatest myths of the twentieth century. Both have become politicized and have shut out those with other science based opinions. Both have exposed the lack of tolerance in the academic/scientific community. Anyone who appears to question these positions is compared to the "flat earth" society. Anyone who seeks to explore design in the universe is shut out of academic circles. Science has become a philosophy, worldview and religion over the last few decades. Woe to those who dare to question, no matter how many PhD's they may have.

This reminds me of a good friend who thought at one time that creation was a myth. Christ changed his life. But before I tell you about him, I need to tell you how I finally came to Fairfield Church.

Discipled in Prophecy

He told them this parable: "Look at the fig tree and all the trees. When they sprout leaves, you can see for yourselves and know that summer is near. Even so, when you see these things happening, you know that the kingdom of God is near. Luke 21: 29-31

The fall meetings at Fairfield Christian Church that I just mentioned were very exciting. We had a guest speaker named Dr. David Reagan.[19] He was a great Bible prophecy teacher. I would lead some worship and then be challenged by his teaching. Having come from a similar background as me, he had spent many years denying the fulfillment of prophecy in the world today. I was somewhere in between theological positions on prophecy. He greatly impacted the elders and opened my mind in fresh ways. His other main thrust was on the need for the Holy Spirit in the life of the church. So the meetings were called Renewal meetings.

Dr. Reagan (no relationship to the president) impacted me and the elders and we all had a fresh perspective on fulfilled prophecy and the place of Israel (the fig tree) in the world today. We have all taught Bible prophecy ever since. No, we were not part of the "eighty-eight reasons why Jesus is returning in 1988"! But Dr. Reagan discipled all of us to be better teachers and leaders.

---

[19] Dr. Reagan has continued to lead Lamb and Lion Ministries ever since we met him.

In the next few months the elders searched for a new pastor and the doors were closing in the church where I was attending. We took a step of faith when the new pastor came and began attending Fairfield. I got to know John[20] and within a few months we did a revival together at his former church. We enjoyed working together and within a few months we were again seeking approval for me to come on the staff.

One last hitch. The day I was to be approved by the board, a foot of snow fell and the meeting was cancelled. The decision was put off a month and I ended up starting in March, 1985, nearly two years after I had first met with Howard. I had just turned 34. Little did I realize I would still be ministering here thirty years later! Guess you could say I was hired twice! I had made many new friends by this time and began meeting several men for breakfast each Friday. While I discipled them some, we discipled each other a lot too.[21]

Frustration to Fruition

A few years of prayer and frustration and faith finally came to fruition. But so did my ministry. **It seemed that finally all my earlier experiences and training came together as I served in worship, adult education and pastoral ministry**. Witnessing, calling on new members, weddings and funerals began to be part of

[20] John Byard
[21] Mark Howes, Norm Anderson, Tom and Mike Milby, and Ron Lowry were early members of that group.

my ministry. Leading worship was a joy. (Even with some frustrations at the earlier church, I had learned a lot about worship there.[22]) I began to play guitar along with our two keyboard players as we did a mix of hymns and choruses. We worked together with our volunteer choir director Susan for the next few years. We started a transition to contemporary worship. A young mother of two began attending. Becky still says that our worship is one of the things that drew her here.

Now for Becky and Jack's story.

---

[22]We would do long worship sets seeking the presence of the Lord in worship, which was a good thing. But one thing I learned about worship is that it is not necessarily the amount of time spent. We could labor over worship until our fingers bled, and some would not be satisfied. I would rather have twenty minutes of well- planned worship in "Spirit and in truth" than forty five minutes that doesn't go anywhere in particular. Most important is to be Spirit-led.

Chapter Three

Jesus Puts Out a Fire

Jack and Becky

We just celebrated Jack and Becky Schumacher's fiftieth anniversary. It almost didn't happen. Their two sons gave wonderful tributes to their mom and dad and how they were raised, from their teen years (and early twenties), in a Christian family.

Jack and Becky were married when Jack was in the Navy. They were only 18 and 16 at the time. Though I didn't know them at the time, they were married by my home pastor in the south end of Columbus. About twenty years into their marriage, their relationship was in trouble. Jack had become a fireman in Columbus and they had two boys. But at one point Jack moved out for nine months. Jack had always been an agnostic, not knowing if there was a God. Becky came to our church and began to pray. A few months later, Jack decided to come home and give it a try. At this point, Becky asked Russell[23] and I to meet with Jack. We both did at different times and talked about faith and apologetics (reasons for the faith). Jack was open and began to find answers to his questions. He accepted Jesus.

Little did we know that Jack would eventually become a Creationist and support ministries that presented the

---

[23] Pastor Russell Johnson

scientific view of Creation. Not only was their marriage saved, but their boys became active in our youth ministry and met the Lord. They both met their wives here at Fairfield. Today, Jack Jr. and Jay and their wives are bringing up their children to know the Lord and are active leaders in two different churches. By the way, they are both firemen as well.

Over the years Jack and Becky have worked with pro-life organizations and also done many mission trips to Mexico. A few years ago, I joined them on three trips and my wife on two. Many people have joined them on these trips, including future deacons and elders of our church. These truly are life changing trips. They have been active on our missions committee for years. We have also shared some family vacations together and Jack and I have gone on several golf trips with other guys from church.

Now that you know their story, you can imagine what a great fiftieth anniversary celebration it was! By the way, they are not that old and neither are we!

From Engineer Ernie to Sheriff Dave

I love hearing our County Sheriff speak in church, which he does all over our county. But I have an even greater joy in knowing how we met and how far he's come. Dave and Loretta have had fruitful ministries over the years since they came to the church. I first met Loretta when she attended here as a single mom. Around that time I also met Dave, a single police officer from Columbus. He started attending our

41

church and I paid a visit to him in his home. Dave had been an officer on the vice squad and had come through a divorce. I encouraged him to be baptized and become a member of the church.

We soon found that this calm, collected police officer had multiple personalities! He loved drama and playing some really whacky characters. One of our pastors, Dale[24], was starting a Sunday morning kids program called Sonshine Crossing. Pretty soon Dave was playing a character named Engineer Ernie.

Dave and Loretta met and married. It was a joy to sing at their wedding. After a few years in our children's program, Dave left the police force and was elected our County Sheriff. He has served our county well and brought both moral and spiritual influence to our community. He's an excellent speaker and preacher. A few years ago, Loretta was moved to help young women who were getting out of jail with no place to go. She founded a ministry called Grace Haven. I remember going to a city council meeting to support her in getting the zoning she needed for this halfway house. Many of these young women have come to our church, and other churches, with Loretta over the years. Some have made decisions for Christ.

Along the way Dave has served as one of our elders. What a blessing they have been to the church. By the way, Dave still loves to act. He played Scrooge in our Christmas production a couple years ago. He has

---

[24] Dale DeNeal now ministers in Danville, Illinois

played a Pharisee in many Easter programs. As I write this, he and I are rehearsing to be Wise Men in this year's Christmas production.

My Kids

Two of the greatest thrills of my life have been the birth and growth of my kids, Matt and Rachel. I'll never forget the first time I held them at their births. I'll never forget the joy of baptizing them several years later. I have been proud of them over the years for following their diverse dreams. We tried to give them a good foundation in the faith and in the church. Both of them played sports through school and graduated from college. Rachel is married with three kids and is a speech therapist.[25] Matt is single and happy to be running a business.

There were several summers of taking them to Christian camp. There were Promise Keepers events and prayer breakfasts with my son. There were family vacations and many trips to Florida to see their grandparents. There have been many good years. There were many good role models for them at Fairfield church. When Rachel married Chris,[26] we gained a great son-in-law. But before that I was blessed with another daughter and son-in-law. That story in a moment.

---

[25] Abigail, Michael and Claire Whitcraft
[26] Chris Whitcraft went to high school with Rachel, but they didn't date each other until college.

Around that time another young couple came into the life of the church with a tough background.

Impossible Odds- Sean and Rachel

Don't let anyone look down on you because you are young, but set an example for the believers in speech, in life, in love, in faith and in purity. I Tim. 4:12

God gets the glory when he helps people overcome their challenges and become successful disciples. Sean and Rachel Frazier have now had two of their three daughters graduate from high school. He has an office cleaning franchise in the eastern part of our state. He teaches adults in his church as their third daughter finishes high school. This is quite a miracle, considering Sean and Rachel both came from broken homes. Survival characterized their teen years more than anything else. For a time, Sean even lived with his mother and sister in a car.

Twenty three years ago Sean came into our Family Life Center for a teen event. He had a pleasing personality and upbeat attitude despite his rough home life. He had a head full of hair (mullet) and wore a bandana. It wasn't long before he and Rachel were the darling couple of the youth group. The church became their family and a stabilizer as their home lives went up and down. They determined to follow Jesus with their lives and their marriage. After high school, Sean became a youth coach. A few years later they became care leaders in our new young adult class. In a few years I would turn the class over to his witty and insightful teaching.

He worked his way up in his company, thanks to discipling from his Christian boss, Jonathan.[27] He went from cleaning offices to managing accounts. He got an opportunity to move and open a new area for his company. Today he has his own franchise and helps his church as well. You never know when there might be a Sean and Rachel in your church or youth group, and the church will make all the difference in their lives!

The Great Interruption

After six years at the church, I faced a crisis. A new pastor had come in the meantime and as we worked together with the youth pastor, the church had been growing. Russell was also in his early thirties when he came. He supported existing ministries and encouraged many new ones to start. Together we made the transition to contemporary worship.

My wife and I had been married seventeen years. We had two children and, though we had some problems, I thought God would always help us handle them. But that was not to be. The most important part of my life was beyond my control. I went through months of turmoil and failed attempts at counseling. When I hit bottom, I found that God was bearing me up on the wings of an eagle. Ultimately, I became a divorced

---

[27] Jonathan Hanks.

pastor. It was a dismal time because I had always believed in the sanctity of marriage and still do. My friends encouraged me to hold on to the promise of Jeremiah 29:11:

> *"For I know the plans I have for you," declares the Lord, "plans to prosper you and not to harm you, plans to give you hope and a future."*

My doctor, elder and friend, Steve Miller had a calming influence on me. My mother encouraged me at this point. She had always had a quiet faith and an uplifting personality. When I wasn't sure what to do, she encouraged me to move on. She helped me and was a stabilizing factor for the kids, who were thirteen and eleven. She was one who continued to believe in me and others did as well.

The church leaders stood with me. **They didn't shoot their wounded, and perhaps it was a test of whether we would really be a "grace place", as our pastor liked to say.** Something therapeutic happened at that time that was really not what I wanted to do. I was "tricked" in to starting a singles support group. The two people who asked me were very insistent, not even knowing about my marriage crisis. I say tricked because they never did show up for a meeting! They ended up getting married within a few months. But God had a plan. I met several new friends at the time that had had their own struggles. We called the group Rebuilders.

Though I remarried the next year, I continued to work with the new group and we had some good adventures together. The group lasted ten years and it was a catalyst for several singles to come into the life of the church and rebuild their lives with Jesus at the center. Some ended up finding new partners that they met in the group and have been married ever since.

Heal me and I will be healed;

save me and I will be saved;

For you are the one I praise.

In you I will not be dismayed. Jer. 17:14

Best Friends

There is a friend who sticks closer than a brother. Pr. 18:24

Let me back up. About a year before my marriage crisis, I met one of my life's best friends. Dan Spires and I had almost nothing in common. He had grown up in the Catholic Church and was a nominal member. (He had been a rather ornery altar boy and had some great stories about that!) He ran a paving business.

One of Dan's sisters and her husband were good friends of ours in our church. They and some other siblings had been praying for Dan to be saved. I met Dan in the parking lot when he was scoping a job for the church. He was a little nervous, but had a pleasant demeanor and loved to laugh. We decided to have some lunches together. He had two little girls and his marriage was in a crisis, partly of his making.

Meanwhile a single mom in our church had met Dan's wife Barb at a local fitness club. Lori was teaching aerobics at the time (and a dental assistant during the day). She had also made a fresh commitment to the Lord just before that time. She began praying for Barb and her little girls that she sometimes brought with her to the club.

I had met Lori and encouraged her to get involved as a new member in one of our Adult Bible Fellowships (ABF). She joined the Lamplighters and was encouraged and valued by her class.

Meanwhile, Dan accepted Jesus anew and was baptized along with Barb. In fact, through witnessing to other family members, Barb's parents and brother were baptized at the same time! What a great celebration! Dan and Barb experienced a healing in their marriage. Dan and I continued to have lunches together and he began to join our Friday morning breakfast when he could.

Just after Christmas of 1990 I entered my marriage crisis. Dan was supportive and encouraging. This relatively young believer lifted my spirits. As he was growing spiritually, my crisis was worsening. He was a prayer partner through my rough days.

Not long after, Lori and I were attending one of our small groups. Later, Dan was one of the first people I told when I began dating Lori. She was my angel when I hit bottom. She believed in me then and continues to support me to this day. But that's another story.

In April of 1992 Dan was my best man when I married Lori. One of my favorite stories is when Dan checked in on Lori and our girls before the ceremony. She had a moment of insecurity and asked Dan if I was still there! He laughed and reassured her that I was very excited about her coming down the aisle! He had a unique laugh which we'll never forget.

We had a great ten years of friendship, went waterskiing and house boating together several times and towed our kids behind his boat. During those years he served as a deacon and elder. He had a special compassion for the less fortunate and went out of his way to help some needy folks. He helped bring the Upward sports program to our church which has been a great community outreach ever since. He and Barb were also supportive of our Christian school. I sang one of his favorite songs at his fortieth birthday: "Somebody's Prayin' for Me"[28].

During those years Dan also had several heart caths and stents and was concerned about his health. I would always try to see him when he was having a procedure. One day I talked with him in the parking lot where we had met. He seemed to have a premonition and was struggling with headaches. I tried to make light of it and cheer him up, but it was obvious he

---

[28] "Somebody's Prayin" by John G. Elliott

didn't expect to see old age. A week or so later he called me and left an odd message. He rambled and then said he'd call back.

A few days later it was Palm Sunday. He had a communion meditation based on one of his favorite songs, "At the Cross- I Know a Place". That evening, while transporting people to and from the building after an Easter cantata performance, he collapsed in the church parking lot with some stroke like symptoms. By the next morning I was visiting him in ICU and he had been diagnosed with a brain tumor. He was aware enough to pray and we prayed in tears. The tumor that was affecting his speech later turned out to be inoperable. So despite surgery and some treatments and much prayer, he went to be with the Lord a few months later.

The favorite song that Dan quoted was one we often sang at communion time:

I know a place, a wonderful place,

Where accused and condemned, find mercy and grace

Where the wrongs we have done and the wrongs done to us

Are nailed there with Him, there on the cross

At the cross, he died for our sins,

At the cross, he gave us life again![29]

It was not easy losing Dan. About a dozen of us all felt he was our best friend. God is faithful. Though He supplies other friends, no two are quite the same. Dan was one of a kind. God's grace was evident in the way his two daughters, in their teens, performed an "expressive sign" number at the funeral service.

Barb later married Bruce, whom she met in the church here. They have been a blessing to each other. Dan and Barb's daughters graduated from our Christian school and today Lindsay, who is a nurse, is in ministry for the Lord. Kelly is working for her parents' paving company.

My Angel

Lori is grateful for her solid Catholic upbringing and has always had reverence for God. However her home life had been dysfunctional and difficult. But as a single mom in her early thirties she began reaching out for more. A small prayer meeting encouraged the participants to seek a personal relationship with Jesus and the Holy Spirit and she was ready.

Then the Lord led her to our church for the next step. One of our pastors helped her get baptized. She found her way to an ABF class and was accepted and encouraged there. The Word of God came alive to her. She saw mature Christian men in the church who were like spiritual fathers and role models to her. She saw

---

[29] "At the Cross" by Randy and Terry Butler

Christian ladies she looked up to. She continued to seek the Lord during her daughter's teen years. A few years later I went through my crisis.

My prayer had been for a partner who was passionate for the Lord and believed in my ministry, and by the time we began talking, I found out that she was both. She had seen enough of life without God in the center. God had prepared both of us for each other and we've had a deep appreciation for His blessing.

God rescued her from some difficult years of a broken family and years of struggling. Once again God had used the body of Christ to reach out to the lonely and struggling. Together with her daughter (in college at that time) and my son and daughter, we began to work on blending our family.

God's Grace is Amazing

Back to the singles group. Shortly after it formed in 1991, my partner in leading the group was Dale Curtis. He and I had some parallels. We were the same age, had each been married seventeen years and had a son and a daughter. We encouraged each other.

We had a great white-water rafting trip that summer with Marian, Arlene, Sharon, Karmen and Susan. After the trip, we had had all the thrills we could handle. Arlene said, "Well, I'm glad I did it, but I'll never do it again!" Others joined the group at various picnics and outings. One time we painted Marian's house. Dale and I played guitar and enjoyed leading worship choruses at meetings. He committed his life to Christ and grew rapidly during that period.

He went through a couple ups and downs and relationships, but we were so happy when he and Marian realized they were soul-mates as well as friends. We had felt that for some time before they realized it. They have been married ever since and involved in the life of the church. Dale has been a deacon, elder and adult teacher. Marian loves to help tend our flower gardens at the church and is one of our great volunteers. She is also a treasured prayer warrior.

Chapter Four

Discipling the Praise Team

Where two or three are gathered, He will be there too

Where two or three on earth agree, He will do what they ask Him to do!

In Spirit and in Truth, in Spirit and in Truth

Jesus said that we would worship in Spirit and in Truth.

In Spirit and in Truth, in Spirit and in Truth

We call upon His name, in Spirit and in Truth.[30]

With musicians, a lot of discipling happens in practices. As our praise band grew, we prayed for God to bring additional guitarists and drummers. At times He answered in a temporary way. But a few have become long-term disciples. **A lot of discipleship is caught rather than taught.** We have had wonderful times of worship where we sensed the Holy Spirit leading and ministering.

Rob Sigler had played in bands in bars and clubs for several years. When he came to our church he discovered that he could play his drums for the Lord! We were so glad to find each other. He has played with me off and on for the last twenty years. He

---

[30] "In Spirit and in Truth" by M. Barbee

played drums on my last CD project of favorite praise choruses. The praise team gave him purpose through the ups and downs of his life—divorce, surgery, and struggling kids. He continues to play regularly. Also, his son is a testimony to God's power and sometimes plays drums for us.

Rocky and Penni came to us out of a more charismatic background and became part of our praise times. Rocky played lead guitar and Penni sang. We would often have two practices a week, one to prepare for Sunday morning, and another just before Sunday night service. Today Rocky helps teach one of our adult classes, as well as playing with the praise band. Penni spent several years working in our youth department and pouring out her love for kids.

Nancy- Wounded Healer

Penni's mom, Nancy Stevens has been a good friend and piano player for many years. She would delight us with her honky-tonk versions of up-tempo songs. She had a great feel for the songs of Andrae' Crouch, Bill Gaither and others. She also has served as one of our administrative assistants.

Nancy's testimony is fascinating. She learned to play piano by ear when she was very young and she has played in church all her life. She was part of our singles group for several years. But nine years ago she was diagnosed with blood cancer (multiple myeloma). Her numbers all went haywire. Parts of her body were beginning to shut down. She wound up in the hospital and at one point her family was told she may only have a couple weeks. She remembers a group of our pastors at that time praying for her in her hospital room. That was another one of those times when we prayed in faith, not knowing the outcome. She was given peace, but more than that, her body began turning around. She has now been surviving and thriving for nine years. Medication has helped her, but God has sustained her! She is grateful to the scores of people who prayed for her and visited her during that time.

In the meantime, Nancy has been a prayer warrior through all the ups and downs of our church family. We have encouraged one another over the years. She continues to encourage those around her and has enjoyed her family, both children and grandchildren, through their growth. She has also played piano for many occasions over these years, even putting on a praise concert with a number of friends. She is learning to "let God set the tempo of her life". Praise God for her testimony! Her life has not been easy, but she is still a wounded healer.

Later some great trumpet players joined us, including Matt Dilger, Doug Cronin and Bob Gillette. Dan Drake blessed us on sax for several years before moving to Florida. These men have been supportive and encouraging of me in several special services and projects over the years.

At other times I have worked with gifted keyboard players. There can be a great camaraderie among members of the worship team. We shared life in many ways during those years. We kept up with the worship and performance music of those times. It is amazing how many anointed worship songs came from that time period.

"Maranatha, Hosanna, and Hillsong"

These were Christian production companies that recorded and published worship music in the nineties. We learned the latest songs from worship leaders like Ron Kenoly, Paul Wilbur, Darlene Zschech and Paul Baloche. Since then, there have been great worship leaders like Chris Tomlin, Laura Story and Kari Jobe. All of these have contributed to the contemporary Christian songbook.

Practices provided many times to pray for one another and the worship life of the church. We often highlighted specific Scriptures for specific worship themes. All of this helps us grow in the Lord. It would take another book to mention all the vocalists that have come through our church and are still good friends. I was worship leader from 1985 to 1997. For the next ten years, I sang in various groups. Then I led worship again in a rotation between 2007 and 2013.

For my first fifteen years here, we also had a wonderful choir under the direction of a volunteer named Susan George. Besides the choir specials on Sundays, we worked together on special music and special programs. For many years she would direct Easter choir and I would direct a Christmas choir or ensemble.

During those years we often had a brother named John G. Elliott come and do worship concerts. We enjoyed his music, which was a combination of contemporary and classical. He played piano, but also wrote and sang his own compositions. He produced albums in Nashville and put together quite a repertoire. One of his more orchestral/choral pieces inspired me to do something very special.

"Let All the Thirsty Come"

Let all the thirsty come, let all the hungry come

Let all who seek for living water find it in the Son

The angels sing his name, and I will do the same

For drawing near to him, we'll find him drawing closer by

Lift up the Lord on high and surely we will find

The bread of heaven fall and living water for us all

Filling our hearts![31]

The song and album of this title were written by John Elliott in the early nineties. On another album he had a song called "Behold the Lamb". As I would listen to the orchestra and dramatic music, I could see Jesus

---

[31] Let All the Thirsty Come by John G. Elliott and Amy Grant

going to the cross-- the whole story acted out before me. Then I got an idea. I called John and asked if he had thought of using that song in an Easter musical. He said no, he had not considered it. I asked if he would mind if I used his music to write a musical. He told me to go for it, and in the next few months I took sixteen of his songs and wove them together to fit the story of Jesus- his preaching, healing, walking on water, sacrifice on the cross and resurrection. And "Behold the Lamb" became the centerpiece as Jesus goes from Gethsemane to the cross. John supplied the music tracks. Wish you could hear it.

Some of those songs fit the story of the apostles going forth from the Day of Pentecost on. So Act Two featured songs about witnessing, praying and trusting God. In 1997, with the help of our choir and drama team, we put the whole thing together and did three performances.

In those days our Family Life center was limited in sound, staging and lighting. But it went well. Many of the guys that I recruited to be disciples were actually friends and disciples in real life. In the musical I played the part of the Apostle James. In the last scene, after my character loses his head, Peter is arrested and sings "Somebody's Prayin" from his jail cell. The story ends with his release by an angel! As great as it was, I hoped someday to do the musical again in the new facility that we built for worship in 1998.

Well, seventeen years passed before the time was right to do it again. In 2014 we did "Let All the Thirsty Come" 2.0. This time we had a larger cast, the choir on stage with us in costume, and all the sound and lights that we needed. Once again we did three performances. The highlight was when John, who had inspired the whole thing, was our special guest and closed out the evening with one of his songs. Once again I played James. My hair and beard were a little grayer this time. Once again, Jesus walked on the water and rescued the disciples while I sang "The Lord Is My Deliverer". We had many wonderful soloists and cast members for this production.

Finishing the Nineties

After we had built the Family Life Center, we were worshiping in there and using it for numerous other activities. We didn't build in a baptistery, so I found a used hot tub. We brought it in and I built the wall and steps to surround it. We were happy to use it dozens of times in the nineties as the church grew.

One of my favorite baptisms was of a young couple named Kirk and Shelly. The unique thing about them at the time is that Shelly was expecting twins. That was February of 1999. Eight years after those girls were born, I got to baptize them!

During those years I became close to my step-daughter Amy. By December of 1999 she was married to Ed Sines. They had met at Ohio University. She became a teacher and by 1999 our first grandson, Aaron had been born. There was some concern that fall about what might happen when the calendar hit January 1, 2000. It was called Y2K. Perhaps all the computers would stop and life would grind to a halt!

It was just unsettling enough that it became a catalyst for Ed and Amy to be baptized. We celebrated their baptisms in the new worship center. Later they had their second son Evan. Ever since, they have been an example in the church and the community through their Christian convictions.

Little did I know I would have the privilege of baptizing Miss Zimbabwe in 2000.

Hellescape and Miss Zimbabwe

Around this time our youth pastor, Matt McGue started an all church program called Hellescape. It was an evangelistic docudrama about the choices we make. It was aimed at young people, but took over a hundred volunteers to make it happen over several weekends in October. We had doctors, nurses, EMS people and several actors of various ages in various scenes around the property.

Dionne was a beautiful young lady with olive skin and multi-ethnic family tree. My son, Matt, called once and said, "I just had a date with Miss Zimbabwe." I wondered if I had heard him correctly. I wasn't sure if he was pulling my leg, which he likes to do. It turned out to be true. Dionne was here in central Ohio on a work visa. She had indeed been chosen Miss

Zimbabwe in her home country a couple years before. She had a picture portfolio to celebrate it.

One afternoon when Matt had brought her to our town, we were having Hellescape that night. She went through the docudrama. It was all about choices, both for time and eternity. The gospel was presented, complete with Christ on the cross. I wondered what Dionne would think. My job was to work in the counseling tent and help with baptisms when people were ready to do that. Sure enough, Dionne came through the door and said in her British African accent that she wanted to be baptized. What a blessing! She stayed in Ohio and ended up marrying another young man. So a couple years later I had the opportunity to do their wedding! God does work in mysterious, exciting ways.

Our church presented Hellescape a total of nine or ten years. It influenced many young people to make better decisions about drinking, driving and drugs. But it also changed hundreds of lives for eternity. Many of the kids who were most blessed were ones who were experiencing discipleship in the youth group and helping put the program on.

Couples in Common

> God has given us different gifts for doing things well...

> ...if you are a teacher, teach well. Romans 12: 6,7. NLT

Phil and Megan

It's not often that you hear of a young attorney leaving her profession to teach at a Christian school. Yet that is what Megan Peters did when our Christian school began. With two children, she gave up some lucrative years to teach here and then be an administrator for about eight years.

Her husband Phil also has a great testimony. As he was earning an educational degree in the seventies, he was influenced by college friends, the Jesus Movement and contemporary Christian music to commit his life to Christ. He became a high school history teacher in public education. He was always supportive of Megan's ministry here. Phil began teaching one of our adult Bible fellowships years ago and the "Bereans" have been discipling folks ever since.

Phil and I have similar tastes in music and our conversations usually include that topic. We have occasionally played guitar together for church sessions.

The Flat Tire

Around the time we met Phil and Megan, we met their friends Kim and Dale Harris. A member of my adult class had a flat tire on our local four lane highway. A young man named Dale stopped to help them and during their conversation he found out about our church. They just happened to be looking for one and already planned to visit with Phil and Megan. Dale and Kim brought their two daughters with them. The first time Dale and Kim came, the man from my class recognized him and said "there's my angel".

We soon found out that Kim had been in a professional dance company. Dale had done a lot of theatrical lighting, including a stint in New York and teaching a class at NYU. Yet, here they were bringing their young daughters to our church in the Midwest. (Kim was working at Nationwide Insurance in Columbus.) Later, they moved to Lancaster and put their kids in our Christian school. Their giftings were to prove very helpful in our production and dance ministries over the years to come. Kim and my wife have also traveled to conferences and concerts in various places to be part of a larger dance ministry.

Since then, God added a son and daughter to their family. All four of their kids have taken part in our Christian school musicals, Christmas and Easter productions and the artistic life of our congregation. Thank the Lord for that flat tire and other Christian friends that invited them.

Let them praise his name with dancing,

Making music with tambourine and harp

Let Israel rejoice in their Maker

The people of Zion in their king.

Psalm 149: 2, 3[32]

---

[32] "Psalm 149- Let Them Praise" by M. Barbee

Believer's Health Insurance

Marc and Tina[33]

Marc is one of my favorite bass players and friends. He hasn't cut his hair since the sixties (or something like that). He played in a lot of bands through his adult years and met Tina in Colorado. He is an electrician who moved with Tina to Lancaster to be close to Tina's folks and start a family. They had a little girl.

When I met them sixteen years ago Tina had just started to come to the church. She found out she needed surgery for cancer. I met Marc in the waiting area of OSU hospital and passed some time with him. We prayed not only for Tina, but for their unborn child who was also at risk. A few months later, Tina was healed and their second daughter was born healthy, Praise God!

Marc began to come to church and got involved in our Sunday morning children's puppet ministry. He also attended my Wednesday night class. One Sunday his puppet character had lines in the script in which he accepted Jesus. Instantly Marc knew that he needed to do the same thing! He became a member and continued in my class.

Since then we have played many worship services and concerts together. A year or so ago, God brought him

---

[33] Marc and Tina Phillips

through heart surgery and he's once again playing bass with the worship team. I like to share with folks that Psalm 103 contains our Believer's Health Insurance policy:

Praise the Lord O my soul;

All my inmost being praise his holy name.

Praise the Lord O my soul,

And forget not all His benefits—

Who forgives all your sins and heals all your diseases,

Who redeems your life from the pit,

And crowns you with love and compassion,

Who satisfies your desires with good things

So that your youth is renewed like the eagle's. Psalm 103: 1-5

Stacie[34]- Passionate for the Lord

God sets the lonely in families- Psalm 68:6

About seventeen years ago, Stacie began attending our church. Before long, this young mother came for counseling and was in the midst of a divorce. We prayed. But as she increasingly committed her life to the Lord, her husband moved the other way and her marriage slipped away. She had great faith and

---

[34] Stacie Blankenship

courage, but also a support network, including her mother. **One of our ABF's adopted her, prayed for and encouraged her as she became the single mother of three.** This class was appropriately named "The Overcomers". The class was older and became mothers and fathers to her in the faith. This class was part of the chain of discipleship. I had recruited and trained the two teachers, who went on to shepherd and teach this class, that went on to adopt Stacie. Praise the Lord.

In a couple years she became an administrative assistant at the church. She became wonderfully involved in missions, pastoral ministry and the local pregnancy care center. She did all she could to set a Christian example for her kids, despite the ups and downs of custody battles. Today her oldest daughter is married to a youth minister.

She had to have heart surgery a few years ago and the church was able to support her through that. Pastor Bill Lavely encouraged her to go to the doctor when she started having symptoms. She is now celebrating five years of health and God's blessings. In the meantime she has gone back to school and finished a degree.

Within the same month our facilities custodial manager Todd Stevens developed symptoms while he was hunting. He went on to have surgery and is also celebrating five years since his recovery.

The next story is a real miracle.

Chapter Five

A Walking Miracle

But those who hope in the Lord will renew their strength.

They will soar on wings like eagles,

They will run and not grow weary,

They will walk and not faint. Isaiah 40: 31

Dr. Tom Rapp and I became friends about twelve years ago. He taught a class entitled "God's Prescription for Healthy Living". After many years in family practice, he saw the benefits of God's plans for healthy eating and living. His wife Toby assisted him in that class. He became an elder and confidant for me. I'll never forget the day, eight years ago, when Toby called to say he'd had an accident, and was in the trauma unit in critical condition.

I felt the realization that I might lose a friend who had become like an older brother to me. I tried to remain calm and prayed as I drove to the hospital. I spoke with Toby and we prayed in one of those rooms off the ER area while Tom was in surgery to relieve the pressure in his skull. He had coded on the way to the hospital.

Tom had been working that morning in the loft of his barn. He somehow missed a step and plunged headlong to the concrete ten feet below. He had a traumatic brain injury and some broken bones. Toby was a woman of great faith who had done lots of mission work and preaching, and who wouldn't give up.

Tom survived through the ICU and Trauma unit and spent two months in the hospital in rehab. He found out later that of the people in the trauma unit that day, he was the only one to survive. We visited Tom in his initial days of being conscious but confused. This was a time when our elders prayed for him in groups and individually. As he began to get better he couldn't put words together but would try to write. It was humorous one day as he was drawing an anatomical sketch as if he was diagnosing a patient—it didn't make sense yet. But over the next few months he made great progress, re-patterning those pathways in the brain and relearning a lot of things. He could eventually say most of the things he needed to.

I can't remember exactly how it happened that he began calling with me. Tom had found out he could no longer practice medicine because of memory issues. (Even though today most of his long-term memory is back and it amazes me what he remembers.) It was about a year after the accident when I asked him to make hospital visits with me on Mondays. He's been my partner now for several years. Many times we've walked into hospital rooms and I've introduced him as a walking miracle. Then he tells his story. I always ask him to pray for the patients after I share a Scripture. To God be the glory!

Years of Testing

"You will seek me and find me when you seek me with all your heart. I will be found by you," declares the Lord, "and will bring you back from captivity."
Jeremiah 29: 13, 14

If you've ever been ahead of God and become overextended, you know what it's like digging out of the hole. In our church's case, it's been several years of debt. In our rush to be a megachurch, we had become overstaffed and overbuilt.[35] Tom's accident came after a tumultuous summer in the life of the church. We had been given a credit line and through some unwise decisions had maxed it out. There were spiritual problems and our lead pastor left. We had a large staff with several experienced pastors, but also a lot of confusion about what to do next. We stumbled for several years, trying different leadership combinations. Many pastors found good positions elsewhere, which solved our overstaffing problem. But every change seemed like a step backwards and people left every time there was a change. We were being severely pruned and tested. Our church of two thousand began to shrink. I once calculated that we had been out of God's will for about seven years. Would it take that long to recover?

We sensed God's discipline and began to wonder when it would come to an end and we would once again have his favor. Once again we're starting on a new

---

[35] We had invested in other off site property and buildings.

path with hopes that it is time for a new season of growth. The church and our pastors have continued to minister over these years, but it has been hard. We're praying more than ever and ready for God's blessings. We're ready to dance again. We have a new lead pastor who wants to work as a team and believes in prayer. Amen.

Musical Interlude with Pastors Three

In the midst of these years of testing, God provided a wonderful escape and ministry opportunity with my co-pastors Tom Alexander and Matt Archibald. Tom became the worship pastor in 1998. Around the year 2000 Matt joined our staff and we realized that we had a true tenor and natural blend. We began learning a wide variety of songs. The joke was that while we had all cut our teeth on contemporary Christian music, we enjoyed singing several gospel songs as part of our repertoire. We sang the old spiritual "Great Gettin' Up Mornin'" *a capella*. We sang songs from The Gaither Vocal Band. But we also did songs from Phillips, Craig and Dean, Newsboys and Newsong. We added our own arrangements of hymns and popular praise songs.

Over the last fifteen years we have sung at a number of churches, a Christian convention, men's meetings, our home Bible colleges, a couple of Christian music conferences, political rallies and funerals. We've all been worship leaders, so our desire has always been to have worshipful concerts. We sing less often since we all minister at different churches now.[36] Last summer we had a reunion concert and had a great crowd. Fortunately, like riding a bicycle, the blend comes back pretty quickly with a practice or two.

Daughters of Zion

Then maidens will dance and be glad, young men and old as well. I will turn their mourning into gladness; I will give them comfort and joy instead of sorrow. Jer. 31: 13

You may think that such a verse from the Old Testament has nothing to do with today. However, I think it contains a principle of blessing. Because Jeremiah 31 also prophesied the New Covenant, I believe this verse is one of the many that describe our joy in the Lord when the New Covenant is operational. **In other words, it's a New Covenant passage in the midst of the Old Covenant.** However, while we're in the age of God's New Covenant in Christ, we certainly can short-circuit it if we're not careful. We can short-circuit it because of worldliness or compromise in the church and thus fail to enjoy all its blessings. We can also short circuit it by religious rules and traditions: "we never did it that way before". Or, if we're not careful, we can divorce ourselves from the Old Testament.

---

[36] Tom at Amazing Grace Christian Church and Matt at Madison Christian Church.

During most of my ministry I believe we have seen a renewal of worship and the arts in the Church at large. It's been a slow process, but very rewarding. Here at FCC, our first step was to add more instruments. Then we realized that movement (dance and expressive signing) could glorify the Lord in many ways. I have seen the Holy Spirit released in many services through the arts. Symbolism that used to be expressed in stained glass is now being expressed in banners. Dramatic presentations have been a great source of blessing to God's people.

We're in the midst of preparing a Christmas musical that includes many elements of the arts, including dance. Joe and Erin are a wonderful young couple who are directing the musical. They have a precious baby named Madeline that is like a granddaughter to us. Lori loves to hold Maddie during long rehearsals. Now let me tell you the story of how Maddie got here!

Joe and Erin's Story

We've known Joe since he was a toddler. He's one of Jim and Sherry Morris's three boys. Now he's in charge of our county's 911 dispatchers. He went to a vocational school for drama and the arts. There he met Erin, a creative dancer and musical drama devotee. Erin started coming to church with Joe. Like so many, her family background had not been very stable. Joe adored her and they were married ten years ago.

Erin soon became part of our fledgling dance ministry, which my wife and Kim had started. Kim, as you might remember from the previous chapter, had had great professional dance experience before getting her "real job". Together the three of them became part of our annual Easter and Christmas productions.

Through a sequence of events we had messianic worship leader Paul Wilbur to our church for a worship concert in 2006. With him came a wonderful dance ministry from Virginia. The Messiah Company soon adopted our girls into their dance ministry and in 2007, our girls and Joe were going to Jacksonville, Florida to be part of one of Paul's worship DVD's. Joe went along and was thrilled at the production and technical aspects behind the scenes. This was the first of many invitations for Erin to perform with Paul and the Messiah Company, including trips to South Korea, Argentina and Mexico.

But one thing was missing for Joe and Erin—a child. They had trouble conceiving and going full term. Many prayers went out for them and eventually some artificial techniques became available. In the fall of 2014 they were going to try again. We stood around the sanctuary during a Messiah Company rehearsal and the entire company lifted up Erin for success. It was a powerful time and step of faith. This time the pregnancy was successful and by June last year little Madeline made her grand entrance into the world. The nurses soon realized that there was an infection problem and sent her to the advanced care Children's

Hospital in Columbus. While we were concerned, we knew God had plans for this little one. Soon she was out of danger and coming home. Praise God.

Why the ten year wait? Sometimes only God knows. But in the meantime Erin has performed many times, directed and choreographed some local church and school musicals, and started her own dance studio, Leaps of Faith. She is training many young ladies and children in all kinds of dance, but more importantly, in character and worship. Her dance recitals are incredible worship services as well as a lot of fun. And yes, this has become another form of discipleship we would not have imagined thirty years ago!

Now, Maddie decided to be born a couple weeks early, the day before last spring's recital. Why was she in such a hurry to get here before her due date? No worry, Joe and Erin's assistants and parents helped the recital to be a total success. But in a matter of hours the doctors were saying that it was a good thing she came early, so that an infection could be discovered and treated. She had to spend only a few days at the hospital. **You can call it Providence or a miracle. Either way, they now have a tiny ballerina.** Maddie is making her presence known at our Christmas musical rehearsals, directed by her mommy and daddy.

Rejoice, rejoice, daughter of Zion

Shout aloud, Israel

Sing rejoice with all your might, O Jerusalem.

(in Hebrew:)

Roni, Roni, bat Zion

Hariu, Yisrael

Simchi V'altsi, B'chol Lev, O Yerushalayim.[37]

Other Forms of Discipleship

Discipleship at a Distance

We all have Paul's in our lives. Some are local and personal. Others are from a distance and may not know us as well as we know them. I have enjoyed listening to various preachers on the radio over the years. In the late eighties I became more familiar with Jack Hayford, from Van Nuys, California. A brother and I drove to Nashville to be part of a renewal conference with Jack as guest speaker. Jack was a Spirit filled pastor who bridged the gap between charismatics and non-charismatics very well. He later became the editor of the Spirit Filled Life Bible (NKJV). I really connected with him. The weekend was great and I met him briefly on the elevator.

A couple years later two other brothers and I went to Los Angeles for a conference and visited Jack's church while we were there. His congregation had been home to some well-known entertainers and Christian artists. It was not a megachurch, but large for the time. We were impressed by his approach on a normal

---

[37] "Roni Roni Bat Zion" by David Loden

Sunday on his home turf. Jack was also a worshiper who sat at the piano to teach us one of his songs. He had just written "Majesty" a couple years earlier and has written many songs since. I guess that's another reason I have always connected with him, since I have been a worship pastor as well as Bible teacher.

In the nineties Jack spoke for several Promise Keepers events and a couple of which we attended with men from our church. I've read a couple of his books. So in those ways I have kept up with him. Now let me digress to another stream which eventually would converge in our lives.

Messianic Melodies

In the mid-seventies I had heard an album by a messianic musician who called his group Lamb. I became aware of a stirring among Jewish people who were turning to Jesus as their Messiah. Joel Chernoff introduced us to some Hebrew words in songs. This all touched me deeply at the time. Over the years we would occasionally do songs in the Hebrew style (minor key). I even wrote a couple. I had also been aware of Jews for Jesus, which was an evangelistic outreach to Jewish people by Jewish people.

Our church hosted David Brickner to do "Christ in the Passover" one year. (Today he is executive director of Jews for Jesus.) We also hosted The Liberated Wailing Wall a couple times. These were Jewish young people who devoted their lives to a music group for years at a time and represented Jews for Jesus. There were always some members of the group who had been ostracized by the Jewish families when they accepted Jesus as Messiah.

So we were primed and ready in about 1996 to hear the music of Paul Wilbur. Hosanna/Integrity music was producing live worship albums. They recorded them in various churches and arenas around the world. They had just produced an album with Paul as worship leader in Jerusalem. This video was dripping with the power of the Holy Spirit, with banners and dance as well as praise band and full orchestra and choir. We watched the "Shalom Jerusalem" video and loved the experience. It had been recorded live in Jerusalem during the Feast of Tabernacles. Our hearts longed to be part of an experience like that. About 1999 we began to have some special praise services where we used some of this music.

Around that time Lori and I went to a "Christ in the Passover" service in Kentucky that featured Paul doing the Seder[38] and the music. Since then, we have hosted our own Passover Seder dinners with the "Christ in the Passover" theme. I believe each one has been an educational and worshipful experience for our congregation. Each one has been an opportunity for our people to get in touch with our Old Testament Jewish roots. We have also taught various "Jewish roots" classes over the years.

---

[38] The Seder is the Passover service and meal.

You may ask "isn't that just Old Testament stuff?" No, it's not required for salvation, but it sure enhances and enriches your understanding of the truths of the New Testament!

The messianic movement was fully joined with the movement to bring arts like dance and banners into worship. We began attending a yearly worship arts conference in Columbus sponsored by Christian Assembly and their pastor, Sam Farina. I had known Sam for over twenty years, going back to my days in the Columbus ministers fellowship. Sam was a loving father in the faith to many and fully embraced the arts. They began having Paul Wilbur perform each year. Our ladies also met many of the dancers who were there for workshops. Many folks from our church attended with us to get a glimpse of "extravagant worship", as Pastor Sam called it. We envisioned having something like that at Fairfield someday. Meanwhile, our church was able to host some significant gospel concerts and contemporary groups. One group that heightened our interest in the arts was Ballet Magnificat.

The Streams Converge 2006-2009

Through a friend in Columbus, Lori and I, along with our senior pastor, had the chance to meet Paul Wilbur. Out of that came our first concert with Paul in the fall of 2006. It was well-attended and a great success. Though we were a large church, we didn't have much of a budget for concerts. So we were thrilled that the

79

budget was met and that we were also able to host the Messiah Company Dancers for the concert. Lori took responsibility for feeding and housing fifteen to twenty guests for these events.

This was the first of almost ten years of having Paul in for concerts. Though at times I felt like I was one of the few carrying this "banner", there was just enough encouragement from others to keep pursuing this. I believe that our congregation has been blessed because we have sought to bless Jesus' brethren "according to the flesh". I must give credit to my wife for believing that God had a purpose, even when I was discouraged.

Through that concert, we really got to know Robert and Connie Wright, from Blacksburg, Virginia. Each year they would bring a dozen or more dancers with them. Connie had had a vision of choreographing Paul's music in the early nineties and God had honored that vision. I have already mentioned how that dance ministry has blessed our people and our dancers.

"Days of Elijah" Comes to Lancaster

These are the days of Elijah, declaring the word of the Lord

And these are the days of your servant, Moses,

Righteousness being restored.

And though these are days of great trials,

Of famine and darkness and sword

Still we are the voice in the desert crying

"Prepare ye the way of the Lord".

Behold He comes, riding on the clouds,

Shining like the sun at the trumpet call.

So lift your voice, it's the year of Jubilee,

And out of Zion's hill salvation comes![39]

How does an Irish worship leader write a song that comes to America through a Jewish worship leader? That's the story of "Days of Elijah". Robin Mark wrote the song in 1996. It was picked up by Paul Wilbur and put on an album in 1999. Since then it has become Paul's theme. Since the song was performed in Jerusalem that year with flags and costumes of the nations, Messiah Company has always performed it with garments representing various nations when they accompany Paul's concerts.

In 2007 Paul wanted to hold a Days of Elijah conference and he chose our church to host it. He invited Messianic teachers to come including Michael Brown, Ron Cantor, and Jeffrey Seif from Zola Levitt ministries. What a great weekend of music, teaching and fellowship that was!

---

[39] Days of Elijah by Robin Mark

Some of our friends had gone to Israel in that season and we prayed about it. We really wanted to go sometime when Paul was going to do a concert, so we waited. Sure enough, in 2009 we heard that Integrity Music was sponsoring a trip to Israel in September, during the Feast of Tabernacles. I shocked Lori when I said, "we're going, even if we have to borrow money".[40] Then Connie called and asked if we could travel with her and eight of the Messiah Company ministry as pastoral covering. That clinched it. Then came the icing on the cake—Jack Hayford was going to be the guest teacher for our tour group! Once again, things were coming full circle for us. We were about to experience the second verse of Days of Elijah:

These are the days of Ezekiel, the dry bones becoming as flesh

And these are the days of your servant, David,

Rebuilding the temple of praise

And these are the days of the harvest, the fields are white in the world.

And we are your laborers in your vineyard, declaring the word of the Lord.

---

[40] A month before we left, we found out Lori had received some inheritance from her Aunt and Uncle which would be a great help to us. The church also blessed me with a significant twenty-fifth year of ministry gift.

Chapter Six

Israel- The Bible Comes Alive

Desert Rain

We were about to board the Boeing 777 in Atlanta airport when I wondered when we would see all the members of our tour group. Then I looked around and there was Pastor Jack with his wife. We saw other faces that we would become familiar with during the next ten days. Once we got to Israel, there would be about eighty, including sixty from all parts of the U.S. and twenty from Brazil. The flight left at 10:30 P.M. and twelve hours later we arrived in Tel Aviv the next afternoon (losing seven hours).

For the first few days we toured the north of Israel, to places like Galilee, Caesarea, Tiberius and Capernaum. We sailed on the Sea of Galilee and walked in the footsteps of Jesus, so to speak. At various stops we would have some music from Integrity musicians and some teaching from Pastor Jack, now aged 75. This was his 39th and possibly his last (so we were told) tour to Israel.

While the top of the old temple platform is currently occupied by two mosques, including the famous Dome of the Rock, we imagined what Solomon's Temple and the Second Temple must have looked like. One of the highlights of the trip (there were many) was Sunday morning service on the southern steps at the base of the temple platform. These steps had been excavated over the last few decades and were the very ones used by Jesus and the disciples. Jesus had probably taught on these stairs (which were carved into the bedrock).

This particular morning we had songs from Paul and devotions from Pastor Jack. Something told me this would be Jack's last time with us. I had a chance to ask him to pray for me and my ministry. Sure enough, it was his last time with us. (Today Jack is retired from his church, but continues to help lead a school for ministers and is very active at age 80+. He was honored in a special edition of *"Charisma"* magazine not long ago.) We also looked at the *mikveh* baths that had been excavated- the place where thousands had been baptized on the Day of Pentecost.

Another highlight was Paul's concert by the Dead Sea. The whole band came from Nashville to help record this live performance. The venue was a parking lot with a stage and several thousand chairs at the Ein Gedi resort. All the Tabernacles tours from Jerusalem came down for the concert. A year later the album was released under the title "Desert Rain". This was a reference to the outpouring of the Spirit that night in the desert. We were very close to where King David had once hid from Saul at the cave of Ein Gedi.

And yet the whole concert nearly fizzled.

Miracle in the Desert

As thousands of people arrived at the concert site, a hundred yards from the Dead Sea, it was over ninety degrees. We met folks from several countries as we were waiting for the concert to begin. But about thirty minutes before start time an announcer told us that the main p.a. system was down. They had just a small channel to make the announcement. A girl played piano and Ana Paola from Brazil sang some praise choruses as we all prayed for the equipment. We found out later that during this interval, one technician was able to change the wiring enough to get the main system up. It went on as scheduled and was a tremendous evening of praise as thousands raised their voices on behalf of Israel: "mountains of Israel, arise, it's time to bring forth new wine, from now till the end of time..." Paul Wilbur led the worship, the band played, the dancers danced, and there were flags representing seventy nations. Messiah Company did the dance for "Out of Zion".

When Paul and the band arrived at our hotel later in Jerusalem, we were eating a buffet together. He shared that the costs of putting on the concert were over a hundred thousand dollars. If it had been canceled, Integrity would have lost a lot of money and the recording project would have been delayed or who knows what. Not to mention about five thousand disappointed people. The Lord came through just in time. I am reminded that in the New Jerusalem we

won't have to worry about p.a. systems. Neither will
the Dead Sea be dead any longer:

> *I saw water coming out from under the threshold of*
> *the temple toward the east...and the water was*
> *flowing from the south gate...He said to me, "This*
> *water flows toward the eastern region and goes*
> *down into the Arabah, where it enters the Sea.*
> *When it empties into the Sea, the water there*
> *becomes fresh. Swarms of living creatures will live*
> *wherever the river flows. There will be large*
> *numbers of fish, because this water flows there and*
> *makes the salt water fresh..." Ezek. 47:8ff.*

There were many other highlights of the trip: seeing
the Garden Tomb and Golgotha (the shape of the skull
is still there); seeing the Dead Sea Scrolls in the Shrine
of the Book, the Wailing Wall, and thousands of years
of history right before us. Along with appreciating
modern Israel, the places of the Bible events came
alive to us. **One person described it as the Bible**
transforming from black and white to color! The
pilgrim gains a sense of geography; mountains, hills,
the main bodies of water, and the history all come into
a new perspective. You gain a sense of what it would
have been like to travel from one place to another.

A significant part of the trip was when Pastor Jack
prayed for my ministry and reassured me that just as
gates had been opened around Jerusalem, so gates
would be opened for my ministry. That prayer also

took place near the steps where Pentecost occurred and the church was born.

Another highlight was seeing the ancient Scriptures found near the Dead Sea in 1947. **I don't think most people realize the significance of the Dead Sea Scrolls.** The main scroll in a building called the Shrine of the Book is that of Isaiah; a complete copy in Hebrew made before the first century. That was a thousand years before the previously oldest manuscript. The text had not changed in those thousand years. The messianic passages like chapter 53 are on display for all Israel to see! (You would have to know where to look because there are no chapter divisions.) But it is also amazing that the scrolls were discovered in 1947, a few months before Israel's rebirth as a nation. Sounds like God's birthday gift to the Jewish people! Any Israeli can walk up to the scroll and read it in his native language, because they all speak biblical Hebrew, which has been restored as their official language!

Just think of these messianic highlights of Isaiah:

Messiah's virgin birth- Isaiah 7:14

Messiah's Deity- Isaiah 9:6- He shall be called...Prince of Peace, Mighty God.

He will be the Branch from Jesse (David's father)- Isaiah 11:1

He will do special miracles- Isaiah 35:5

Servant for God for both Jews and Gentiles- Isaiah 49: 1-7

The Servant (Messiah) Obedience in Suffering- Isaiah 50: 4-9

The Messiah's Substitutionary Sacrifice, Death and Resurrection- Isaiah 53

All of these marvelous Scriptures are more accessible to Israel than ever before.

More Testimonies

A Modern Dorcas- Pat

In Acts 9: 36 we find the story of Dorcas. She was a friend of widows and made clothing for the needy. She became sick and died. Her widow friends sent for Peter. He came, prayed for her and raised her from the dead.

This story reminds me of a widow in our church who teaches a Bible class and does good deeds by mentoring other women. A year ago I visited her class one Sunday. She seemed fine. Little did I know that two days later she would be fighting for her life. Pat[41] asked for prayer for a headache that Sunday and I'm sure we all prayed for her.

Less than forty-eight hours later she suffered a perforation in her abdomen and infection was spreading. She was quickly taken into the first of

---

[41] Pat Schindler

several surgeries. She coded a couple times and had to have her heart restarted. Once, her heart had stopped for four minutes. The first few times we visited and prayed she was sedated and hardly knew we were there. She was near death on a couple of occasions. At times like this we pray and try to trust the Lord, not knowing the outcome.

There were many hospital visits from family and friends and pastors. She spent thirty-one days in the hospital before being transferred to a rehab center for seven weeks. She was finally strong enough to return to her home. A few months later she was able to be back in church. Today she is fully recovered and teaching her class again. Her class has prayed and encouraged her all the way. Today, at 75, she still loves teaching. You're never too old to share the love of God and His Word. **Her doctors have used the words "amazing" and "miracle" to describe her survival and recovery. Sure seems like a resurrection to me!**

Another Hellescape Story- Glen

We were reminiscing with a good friend Carol Starner recently in the church foyer. I asked her to remind me how she and Glen, her husband, had come to the Lord and to the church. She had started coming to church, and praying for her husband to come to know the Lord. He had grown up with godly parents, but had been a partier for several years. He had shoulder length hair.

So he happened to be in the church one of his first times here and our Easter musical director said "We need your hair, would you be in a scene in our Easter production?" I guess Glen couldn't say no and he ended up being one of the thieves on the cross. Across from him, the other thief was a guy with whom he used to party! Does God have a sense of humor or what! Of course, Jesus was in the middle. I don't remember which thief went to Paradise that day (in the play), but both of them ended up getting saved.

Glen began to be discipled by the church in various ways. A couple years later he was recruited to be Jesus at the crucifixion scene in Hellescape. He would spend all evening running the scene twenty or more times in a barely heated tent. In between scenes of hanging with only a loincloth, he would wrap in a blanket and hug Carol to try to get warm. What a sacrifice! There is no telling how many hundreds were impacted by that scene.

In 2002 Jack Schumacher recruited him to go to Mexico with us and it was my first mission trip. It was a delight to get to know Glen better and see his spiritual growth. He was a jack of all trades and very helpful in the building projects we worked on in Nuevo Rosita, Mexico. He has become the spiritual leader of his home, his wife and two daughters. He has served the church now as a deacon and an elder. He is always looking out for the least and the lost, remembering how lost he was a few short years ago.

I should not forget that his sister and his parents were also praying for him. His sister, Lu Fox, was one of our administrative assistants for several years. I got to know the family better over the years as we had the funerals for their parents. It was a special privilege to share our holy land trip with their father Bob just a few months before he died. I'm sure he had New Jerusalem on his mind a lot in those days. What a joy to see another family impacted by the gospel and the church family.

The Holy Spirit surely deserves all the credit for moving people in the right place and time to say and do things that will impact others beyond their imagination. He weaves an amazing tapestry among various people and personalities to bring about wonderful results. He can network far beyond our ability to try to connect people who might be good for each other. I love it when God does these things! Carol gives special thanks every time her Glen gets up to share a communion/offering meditation, as he did the day we shared. Hallelujah!

How sad that so many believers miss out on the blessings of discipleship and fellowship with believers in the church. They believe the lie that they can serve God and grow on their own without the church. They usually end up growing in the wrong direction— growing farther from the Lord, not closer. On the other hand, it's exciting when people pray a simple prayer to find the small group that they can relate to, or the mentor that they long for. God will open those doors if we're patient. **We also have to be willing to**

try more than once. Perseverance pays off. People eventually find the class or group that fits. God may unexpectedly provide the Christian friend or mentor that they're looking for. But we have to be willing to wait on His timing. What's the worst thing that can happen if you don't hit it off with the first individual or couple or class that you try? You've made more friends in the life of the church! You also may be blessed by a friend that you never expected or didn't think you had anything in common with. That has happened to me more than once!

Jay and Terri[42]

I have to credit my fellow pastor Dale for reaching out to Jay some twenty-three years ago. Jay had an addiction problem. Dale patiently encouraged him in the Lord and was there for him on several occasions. Jay became involved in our sound ministry, which he did for over twenty years. We worship leaders aren't much without good sound men! We often ask for more of a certain voice or instrument in the stage mix. We are always tweaking and they have amazing patience. One of my favorite tee shirts was when a sound man wore one that said "More talent in the monitor, please".

When Dale left our ministry a few years later, Jay and I began to get together for lunch and encouragement. He had done very well, but occasionally the old ways would try to drag him back. When Jay retired, I invited

---

[42] Jay and Terri Stump

him to make visits with me every Thursday. This was a blessing to him and a relief for his wife! For almost ten years he was my partner and we made a great team. He also continued to help in the sound ministry for weekly and special programs. There were times when I didn't know what Scripture or prayer to give him, but God worked through the ups and downs. He also developed a heart for ministry and prayer for others! God has preserved him and his marriage through the body of Christ. They became very close to their ABF class and teacher, Ken Brooks, who shares a love of horses with Jay and Terri.

Eventually Terri retired and we got closer as couples. Thanks to Dale, his teacher Ken Brooks and many friends and care team leaders, Jay and Terri continue to serve the Lord in their retirement. For a year they worked at an RV park in North Carolina. Once again, Jay found himself running sound in a small country church! They also get our **eprayer** prayer requests and pray for those in need.

Another Widow Story

Diana[43] lost her husband in her early sixties. She had been so devoted to him that after his passing she was lost. Her life became more difficult and finances were tight. But a lady friend reached out to her and invited her to church. Donna also asked me to visit Diana and I did. Today, she sent me a testimony of how God has blessed her in the last two years. Her husband died

---

[43] Diana Lax

just two years ago and she started coming to church a few months later. Before long Donna convinced her to come into their ABF. About the same time, she recommitted her life to Jesus and was baptized. Her testimony includes several people reaching out to her, the sale of her house and God leading her to a more affordable situation. Then she was having some health problems and God is healing her from that. The Lord also provided an experimental drug program to help her handle her diabetes at less cost.

In less than two years, Diana has a church family, her needs met, and a new purpose for living. Now she wants to be an angel for someone else like others have been to her. Praise the Lord. What a wonderful example of the body of Christ working as a team to help someone find their way. She has a big grin on her face every Sunday.

John's Identity Lost and Found

Ardella had been praying for her husband for several years to recommit his life to Christ and come to church. John[44] was a good, hard working husband and father. But a few months ago his identity was stolen and it caused him to become depressed. He had some rough weeks. We had a visit, along with members of Ardella's adult Bible fellowship, and prayed for his healing and restoration. At that time he looked like the world had fallen in on him and he even looked physically ill. A few days later he was in church with a

---

[44] John and Ardella Campbell

big grin. Before long he was telling me he wanted to be baptized! In a few weeks he was baptized along with his teenage grandson. Now he is here every week with an even bigger grin on his face. What a transformation!

Chapter Seven

Principles that Have Helped Us

I believe in Bible doctrines. Doctrines are simply all the verses that have a bearing on a certain subject. Paul distinguished between doctrines that were helpful and those that were doctrines of men.

Paul told Timothy to avoid;

> ...whatever else is contrary to the sound doctrine that conforms to the glorious gospel of the blessed God, which he entrusted to me...Watch your life and doctrine closely. Persevere in them...for the time will come when men will not put up with sound doctrine. I Tim. 1:10, 4:16, II Tim. 4:3

There are broad areas of doctrine that we call essential. We must agree on these broad areas: the Three in One, the Deity of Christ, Authority of Scripture, and Plan of Salvation. **There are other areas of opinion that have been debated by church leaders for centuries.** I have encouraged teachers and others to use sound principles of interpretation to arrive at conclusions. We have encouraged them to practice unity and love in all things.

Some doctrines have been neglected from time to time; others have been overblown, depending on which brotherhood you are part of. In a non-denominational church, it has been interesting (to say the least) to see how folks come together from various backgrounds to reason through the Scripture.

Some doctrines are found in both Old and New Testaments: the Nature of God, the Nature of Man, Law and Grace. The Doctrine of Christ (the Messiah) is hidden in the Old and revealed in the New. The work of the Holy Spirit is hinted at in the Old and fully revealed in the New. In fact, Ezekiel said that the new covenant would be a covenant of the Spirit: Ezekiel 36: 27 says *And I will put my Spirit in you and move you to follow my decrees and be careful to keep my laws.*

Doctrine vs. Theology

To my thinking, Theology (the study of God) is important, but tends to be a study of what people say <u>about God.</u> Doctrine is more about letting the Scriptures speak for themselves. That has been our goal. Some would say we have done well: others may disagree. As a church we've been labeled Liberal by some and Legalistic by others. I hope that means we're close to where we need to be. Both extremes are ditches we try to avoid. I always encourage teachers and others to share their convictions, but not be dogmatic or reject those who disagree.

With any doctrinal issue, it is possible to construct your argument with Scripture and then extrapolate to conclusions beyond Scripture. In mentoring our teachers over the last twenty-five years, we have tried not to do that.

We believe that there is room for opinion (liberty) in several areas. With that being said, I believe that at times we have quenched the Holy Spirit in favor of programs and human effort, rather than rely upon Him. We have run ahead of the Holy Spirit, instead of really laying ideas on the altar and waiting on God. We have paid the price for this. In a season of discipline we have been forced to rely on God for weekly and monthly provision for the church. May we move forward with a firm reliance on the Holy Spirit:

> *Not by might, not by power, but by my Spirit says the Lord. Zech. 4:6*

Rightly Dividing the Word

II Timothy 2:15

This principle includes knowing the main divisions of the Old and New Testaments and their purposes. But it goes beyond that to principles of interpretation. Most Bible teachers through the centuries have advocated a few (between 5 and 10) principles that will help Bible students arrive at similar conclusions. Here is a brief list[45]:

> *Faith in Jesus as the Son of God*
>
> *Respect for the Bible as the Word of God*
>
> *Harmony between various books and passages*
>
> *Literal as intended*

---

[45] From Dr. Lewis Foster of Cincinnati Bible Seminary

Figurative if obvious

According to Context

Guidance of the Holy Spirit

According to Emphasis (Balance)

Verification with study resources

Application to Self

While the secular world points to dozens of differences of practice across the body of Christ, it is amazing how close we can be in agreement if we follow these basic principles. Most believers have learned that our differences are far outweighed by our agreement in major beliefs. Thus believers from a wide variety of backgrounds are able to worship together.

The Sabbath Principle

We need to be more aware of the Sabbath principle in the Scripture. God created us to rest on the seventh day and also to let our fields rest the seventh year. What does that part have to do with ministry? Every minister/pastor/disciple needs to rest a day a week, but many violate this principle. Moreover, what about the seventh year? We are not farmers, after all! But what if we looked at our programs from a Sabbath perspective? A field might compare to a program. What if we purposely reexamined our programs every seventh year and let them rest a year?

Here are some examples from our history. We had a wonderful outreach program called Hellescape, as I have already mentioned. Did we run it too long? After six or seven years it lost its luster. Yet no one wanted to let it rest. We finally did, but not when it was at its peak. You see, it takes faith to let a successful program rest, even for a year. Christmas and Easter programs are like that too. For a few years, we ran many of our key workers ragged, running from Christmas to Easter to Hellescape in the fall and back again to Christmas! All were major programs that took weeks of preparation/performance and dozens of volunteers. When volunteers can't say no, they sometimes leave the church to catch a break! We burn lots of weekends and years because it's hard to say "no". Singers, sound techs and drama people often get caught in these endless cycles.

Oh, by the way, this was all in addition to the regular services fifty-two weeks a year! **Finally, someone said, let's do <u>one</u> of these special programs each year, and of course at different times of the year**. Excellent!

Besides, do you remember the 20/80 rule? 20% of the people do 80% of the work. It's the 20% that get caught in the endless cycle. Others will help occasionally and there is certainly value in that. The rest will cheer from the sidelines and wonder why you're not doing more!

What if we changed our formats every seven years? Would that bring some fresh ideas from the Holy

Spirit? What if we gave ministers a sabbatical? That doesn't necessarily have to be a whole year every seven, but some significant amount of time—a semester to take a class, or teach in a different venue. This would also force other disciples to step up and fill gaps and make us less dependent on key people. Would this take faith? Of course! But that's what God blesses, steps of faith.

Our church does require some volunteer leaders like elders and deacons to rotate off after three years for at least a year. Did I hear some "Amens" on that? However, we're not consistent with other ministry leaders doing that.

While I did not take a sabbatical from leading worship after seven years, circumstances intervened after thirteen. I was losing my voice each week until we hired our full-time worship pastor. (Interestingly, after eight years or so, he was getting burnt out as well.) After Tom took over as worship pastor, my voice went through a much needed rest and healing over the next year!

Perhaps the Sabbath principle has worked in my life without my consciously applying it. Though I have been in the same church all these years, many of my duties have rotated back and forth. As I mentioned, I had breaks from worship leading. I had breaks from leading our ABF teachers while other pastors helped in that. While I have always done forms of pastoral ministry, these have varied. I have always covered hospitals at least two days a week, but other pastors have certainly helped take the pressure off doing it all.

In the last ten years I have done more funerals than ever, but that is not burdensome to me. Each one is a unique opportunity to minister, and to focus on eternal truth. Other staff pastors have done their share.

The Bible- Still a lamp to my feet and a light for my path!

The Bible might have seemed fifty feet tall to me when I was a kid. Now it's 5,000 feet tall. It is a mountain of wisdom, life lessons, faith instructions, and the key to God's heart. **It is revelation from God, not the ideas of men**. One author called it "a moral miracle" because it was so far ahead of its time.

The *Halley's Bible Handbook* was given to me when I was in sixth grade. I still use it (in a later, nicer edition). Like my old mentor, Art Scott, I still like to "rightly divide the word of truth" as II Tim. 2: 15 (KJV) commands us.[46]

But how is the Church doing in the knowledge of God's word? Not too well, I'm afraid. We've made it too easy to be a Christian. We've set expectations too low for learning God's Word. How many of us have memorized the names of all the books of the Bible? How many understand the different types of literature

---

[46] I believe that all the modern translations have something to offer and that they should be compared with one another.

within the pages of the Bible. Do we really treat it as "Basic Instructions Before Leaving Earth"?

With the translations we have today, most kids at age 14 or 15 should be able to read through the Bible or at least a modified program where you read one chapter a day for a year. It's okay to skip some hard parts. Why not start with the New Testament, which is easier to understand? Of course, the larger problem is that we're so device oriented that people are not reading anything but their devices. Even then, you can get Bible programs to make it convenient.

But the Bible program will not help you see the overall divisions of God's word, like holding it in your hand will. People are not likely to underline, earmark pages, or carry the Bible with them. How about the sheer distraction of emails, tweets and you name it, beeping on the phone every few seconds?

The Bible is still holy, and should be set apart as such. That's my two cents. Everyone should read the Gospels and know how they compare and contrast with each other. We should know why there are four versions of Jesus' ministry and how they each give us additional insight into the Master. (That's called harmonizing the gospels. Tatian was the first Bible teacher to do that in 150 A.D.!)[47]

The Jesus of my childhood has not changed. Yes, I know him from an adult perspective, but He hasn't

---

[47] *The Diatessaron* by Tatian.

changed. I know him as the Word made flesh, in His deity, His glory and His omnipotence. Yet, I learned most of that from hymns as a kid. Yes, theology class changed my understanding, but not him. Yes, philosophy class changed my understanding of him in relationship to other gods and systems, but it didn't change Him.

During communion as a teen I sometimes imagined Jesus stretching out his arms over our people. I still imagine that today. He is approachable. He is as close as a prayer. Now I have learned that through unexpected twists and turns in my life. I don't know how I would be where I am today without his ever present help in times of trouble.

I am thankful for Christian friends and their wonderful testimonies in their ups and downs of life. I pray that Jesus will be as real to my grandchildren as he has been to me. There are more distractions than ever before. The accessibility of sports and entertainment can be a constant distraction from the most important issues of life. They will need Him in the moral, emotional, and intellectual challenges of life.

Discipleship Through Writing

An important part of discipleship is making the Bible come alive to people. God led me in a unique way over the last dozen years to do just that. One year while singing in the choir for an Easter musical, the Lord began to stir my imagination. I was focused on the Apostle John. As I watched his character in our drama, I began to rehearse the things I knew about him- his time with Jesus; his later years in writing the gospel, letters and Revelation; his long career in the early church. The idea for a historical fiction book began to develop.

Over the next few months, I wrote during times of inspiration. It became a fictional memoir of John, with him recalling how he wrote about his experiences. I added some fictional conversations with other disciples and apostles as they reminisced about their time with Jesus. I quoted important passages of Scripture as John "wrote" them. After a few months, I realized that what I had written was one third Bible, one third history, and one third imagination. (With a little room for what felt like revelation to me.) It became *The Journal of the Apostle John*.

I was disappointed over the next few months to see how tough the Christian publishing field was. Major publishers would not even accept unsolicited manuscripts. So with the help of the church, I self-published several hundred copies. Most of those became hospital gifts and texts for classes that I taught. The proceeds from the ones that we did sell went back into printing. And so the book became a teaching tool.

For my next book I decided to tackle Matthew in a similar fashion. Only this time the Lord gave me a fictional modern character for the introduction. Matthew's manuscript was to be discovered by my fictional professor of ancient languages, Matt Burns from Columbia University, who was initially a skeptic. This one was called *The Meditations of Matthew Levi*. This book was to be more authentic with first century Hebrew names as proper nouns. Jesus was Yeshua, John was Yohannon, and so on. This time, Matthew was dictating his gospel to his young disciples who were copying it. There are times for questions, reflection, and interaction between Matthew and his students. The book was finished late in 2003. Fortunately, I had a friend at church who was an artist and did a cover for me. What a blessing.

Over the next couple years I had ideas for Mark and Luke. Each book developed unique fictional characters along with the Bible characters. Mark witnesses to a young pagan couple in Rome while he visits Peter in prison and writes his gospel. Luke visits Jerusalem as a child and becomes captivated by Jesus of Nazareth. Later he writes his gospel as he interviews eyewitnesses in Jerusalem.

Each book became an opportunity for a Bible class and for me to introduce students to the various gospels. Which one is my favorite? Whichever one I'm working on at the time! Eventually, I added a book on Acts called *Searching for the Bride*. In that one, my fictional professor, Matt Burns, became more prominent. In the last five years I have done a short book on Israel: *The Twentieth Century Miracle.* That was followed by a book called *A Twenty First Century Look at the Old Testament.* After years of teaching Old Testament

Survey classes, I was inspired to write a semi-survey, semi-commentary, with my fictional character leading the exploration. He ties the Scriptures in with modern day worship, fulfilled prophecy, and even a trip to Israel. He deals with the objections of liberal skeptics over the inspiration of Scripture. In some sense, it's a reflection of my own journey of discovery over the years. The Old Testament comes alive to Matt Burns, his wife, and hopefully, the reader.

Teaching Teachers

Greg Elliott is a professor of astrophysics. Twenty some years ago he was a member of our college/career class. I helped recruit him to teach the class and began to have breakfast meetings with him. He was brilliant and lovable at the same time. Very laid back in some ways.

His wife Jeanette was an energetic overcomer. She had lost a leg as a child in a bicycle accident. But it didn't slow her down. She could do about anything she set her mind to, including volleyball, and many sports. She had great faith and became a physical therapist.

Together, Greg and Jeanette led our college group for several years. Then they moved to the east coast where Greg taught at an Ivy League college for many years.

During that season, J.T. Burcham met Karen in the College/Career group and they got married! Today they are still serving full time in the life of our church and Christian school. J.T. is a media teacher and coordinator. Karen is a coordinator for our preschool after several years with the elementary school.

The Defenders Class

My first attempt to start a "young marrieds" class had some humorous results. One couple came that was in their forties. Another couple that showed up had white hair- they missed the part about "young". So the Defenders class ended up being a little older than I had anticipated. (About fourteen years later we started the young marrieds' class I spoke of earlier.) Thankfully, Bill and Margaret Hines stayed with the Defenders class and he has been teaching it the last dozen years or so. Bill and I have enjoyed our friendship in the class and as fellow teachers and elders over the last dozen years. Don Redwine has also come along to help teach.

Teacher Fellowships

Over the years I have tried several ways to encourage our teachers with principles and ideas for teaching. We brought in some of my favorite professors and friends to discuss biblical content and presentation. We often did this at a yearly banquet to thank the teachers and encourage them. When we don't have a banquet, we have a teacher's summit meeting on a Saturday to present new information and challenges.

I have also met one on one with most of our teachers to hear from them how things are going. We have talked about a wide range of challenges over the years. One of my favorite topics is managing classroom time between social time, prayer time and lesson time; balancing lecture and discussion.

For classroom time, I've suggested things like a 20/20/20 minute balance between elements listed above. A lot of teachers (and students) prefer shorter times for social and prayer to allow more time for lesson and discussion. All these factors are important for a class to bond. Class members also need time outside of class to bond with one another, through service projects, socials, or home Bible studies. Many classes have been creative in their activities.

Adult Bible Classes have strengthened our church over the years, especially through the ups and downs with ministers. Lifelong friendships have been forged in these classrooms and beyond.

A Class of Overcomers

At one point we had a teacher training class and I asked two men to work together on a class. It was an unlikely combination of personalities, but both men had overcome adversity in their lives. Ron and Donna married after tragic first marriages. [48] Donna came out of an abusive situation. She and her two daughters survived some rough years. Ron's wife had died in a

---

[48] Ron and Donna Weisenberger

car accident, leaving him with four sons. Together they forged a blended family and experienced God's healing.

Joe and Trish[49] had just lost an older son in a work accident. They were overcoming their own pain when the class came together. Together, the two couples helped and encouraged many folks in the last fifteen years to be "overcomers". They have "adopted" a variety of single folks and couples over the years. No doubt, the adversity these couples had faced gave them compassion for the lonely and struggling. By the way, it was this class that reached out to Diana in the story above (and Stacie a few years before that).

> *Praise be to the God and Father of our Lord Jesus Christ, the Father of compassion and the God of all comfort, who comforts us in all our troubles, so that we can comfort those in any trouble with the comfort we ourselves have received from God. II Cor. 1: 3-5*

Helpers Train Leaders

The Helpers Class is one of our long running classes. Taught for many years by Ken Brooks and Tom Johnson, they have trained and discipled many of the adults in our church. They continue to raise up other teachers from within the class. Ken is one of our resident prophecy teachers and sometimes teaches two classes a week. Their class has also cared for

---

[49] Joe and Trish Gormley

many senior adults in homes or nursing care over the years. I have heard more than one person say that Ken is the reason they are still a part of our church family.

Prayer Partners

I have been blessed and encouraged by some special prayer partners over the years. Randy[50] was one of our teachers for many years that joined me early one day a week to pray over the needs of the congregation (primarily requests on our communication cards). He helped me a great deal. **Most of what I've learned about prayer I've learned from actually praying with people and hearing them pray.** Besides, it's much easier to pray over lists of requests when you have a partner. When you run out of things to say, your partner can help you.

Of course, it is the role of the Holy Spirit to help us pray when we don't know exactly what to pray (Rom. 8:26). Over the years Bible teachers have also taught a lot on prayer. For example, to use the Lord's Prayer as a pattern and guide for prayer that can be expanded upon. We have had many sessions over the years where we have prayed for an hour just expanding on the model prayer that Jesus gave us. I have tried to teach many disciples that pattern over the years and challenge them to expand their prayer lives.

We learned a lot about corporate prayer over the years from prayer meetings, prayer weekends and you

---

[50] Randy Benedetto

name it. I learned a lot from the corporate example of Jim Cymbala of the Brooklyn Tabernacle. We got to visit one of their weekly prayer meetings in 2002. By the way, they are known for their incredible choir that was built up through prayer over many years. God has used Jim and his wife Carol as a reminder to the body of Christ of the centrality of prayer. He always said, "don't judge the spirituality of a church by Sunday morning, but by their prayer meeting". Most of us are found wanting by that standard!

Walt and Becky[51]

Another couple that has been with us for twenty-five years is a great example of prayer. Becky has been a prayer warrior since before Walt was saved. She challenged him to come to church with her as an example to their daughters and he did. They run a business and have tried to follow God in their endeavors.

A few years ago Becky began to send prayer requests to five other people. Eventually, the number grew to nearly a hundred that receive regular requests on email.

Walt went on to serve as a deacon, elder and currently a leader of our safety team. Becky continues to encourage others through the eprayer ministry. They have encouraged their children and grandchildren in the Lord!

---

[51] Walter and Becky Beatty

Failures

Yes, there have been some. I don't want you to think that discipling is always easy or natural. But failure isn't final. Perhaps some of these friends were not meant to mentor with me. A few didn't trust me or weren't ready to receive input. Or I was simply not the one with whom they could relate. I don't blame them because I am certainly not perfect. Some of our relationships were derailed by events in the church that were beyond my control. But just because a certain relationship doesn't work out is no reason to quit seeking discipleship.

After all, John Mark's first attempt to work with Paul didn't work out. He left Paul in the middle of a mission journey. Paul did not want to take him on the next one. Yet, Barnabas reached out to him. He was better off with Barnabas and Peter for a few years. And yet, years later, Paul said that John Mark was "useful" to him.[52] I trust that many relationships that were very short have helped some John Marks to be useful in other ministries.

It is important to allow God to use you in someone's life, even if it is only for a few months and doesn't turn out as you hoped. Sometimes you are a bridge. A few of the folks I have encouraged have gone on to fruitful ministry in other places. Failure isn't final. Fellowship is fluid!

---

[52] II Tim. 4: 11

Are there any helpful tips when someone leaves? First, pray and let them go. One thing I've learned is that people who have to be carefully kept, can't be. Secondly, bless them if you can. You may not be able to bless bad attitudes or problematic personalities, but you can let them know that you will pray for them and keep the door open. Sometimes they do come back.

Chapter Eight

Generations of Disciples

Two young men that I worked with briefly when I first came to Fairfield are now in ministry together. It seemed unlikely for Joel and Shawn[53] at the time. I hired them to paint my mom's house before they were sixteen. Some of the paint actually ended up on the house! But we spent some time in a small "praise team" learning a couple songs. They didn't have an overabundance of talent at that time, football being one of their priorities. Our youth minister, Jeff, did a lot of discipling with them in their early years.

Years later Joel had learned guitar and was back in town planting a congregation. He would play guitar and then step out to preach! Shawn joined him and they continue to pastor the local Vineyard church. . By the way, Shawn's dad was the one who visited me when I was making my decision for the Lord at age eleven!

Joel and Jason[54] are two other young men who grew up in our church. Joel's mom sang in an ensemble I had. Sometimes he would tag along and ask to play my twelve string guitar. Eventually Rocky took him under his wing and taught him a lot about guitar and worship, leading our teen praise band. Joel went on to Bible College and now is back in our church as worship

---

[53] Joel Seymour and Shawn Banker
[54] Joel Reid and Jason Morris

pastor, leading worship every Sunday. He is a talented singer and guitarist. Rocky often plays lead guitar as Joel is leading. I had once worked to include Rocky in our praise team so now we see a second and third generation of discipleship as Joel leads others. Not only that, but Joel is also leading the Christian school praise band, along with Sue[55], one of our other worship leaders. The beat truly does go on! Thankfully, when Joel returned to Fairfield as a pastor, he brought his wife Randi and she is our Children's Ministry Director.

Similarly, Jason grew up here as I led worship and later under Tom Alexander's leadership. Jason's talent emerged in high school as both a singer and keyboard player. He played with a young contemporary group under Tom's encouragement. Jason majored in business and works for the government, but he has already helped two or three churches by leading worship part time. I was blessed to help coordinate both Joel's and Jason's ordination services.

Paul's Lessons to Timothy

There are many principles in Paul's pastoral (discipling) epistles. We have referred to some of them. But others that deserve mention are accountability, purity, correct doctrine, and order in the church.

Paul gives lessons on worship: "I want men everywhere to lift up holy hands in prayer, without

---

[55] Sue Johnson

anger or disputing." Have we reached that goal in our congregation yet? No, not with the majority. But we continue to try to set the example of worshiping in spirit and in truth, and praying fervently. Men should be leaders in worship, not passive spectators. Leaders should set the example.

> *"...But set an example for the believers in speech, in life, in love, in faith, and in purity."[56] These things will never go out of style. There is nothing worse than moral failure in pastors and church leaders. The moral failure of several high profile television preachers in the 90's has hurt the credibility of all ministers. No matter what we do to communicate with our culture, we should not let down our guard in these areas. We are to be in the world, but not of the world. Paul's advice to "treat the older women as mothers, and the younger women as sisters, with absolute purity"[57] has always helped me. Now I can add the phrase, "treat them as daughters and granddaughters"!*

Conversely the women in our churches still need teaching about modesty and virtue and what that means about styles of dress. Women can help or hurt the men in the church by how they dress. Many have no filters from their upbringing, and some filters are needed.

---

[56] I Timothy 4:12
[57] I Timothy 5:2

Women have been mentoring women at FCC for several years. Titus 2 says that older women are to teach the younger and that has happened in several instances. Our current women's ministry leader, Lisa Kandra, was discipled by one of our earlier children's directors, Donna Smith.

Paul also said "for physical training is of some value, but godliness has value for all things…" In my forties I retired from church basketball and softball, but in my fifties I began jogging. That has been a tremendous help to me in many ways. It has helped as an outlet for stress and helped protect my sanity during the ups and downs of ministry.

Paul's second letter to Timothy contains some powerful warnings and prophecies. One warning is to **never forget the inspiration of Scripture: that it is "God Breathed" and useful for teaching, rebuking, correcting and training in righteousness."**[58]

Paul warns twice about the "later times when some will abandon the faith and follow deceiving spirits, and things taught by demons".[59] Again he says, "there will be terrible times in the last days. People will be lovers of themselves, lovers of money, boastful, proud, abusive, disobedient to their parents, ungrateful, unholy, without love, unforgiving, slanderous, without self-control, brutal, not lovers of the good, treacherous, rash, conceited, lovers of pleasure rather

---

[58] II Timothy 3:16
[59] I Timothy 4:1

than lovers of God—having a form of godliness but denying its power,"[60] "for the time will come when men will not put up with sound doctrine".[61] It is obvious that we see all these things played out on television without even leaving our homes.

A New Original Sin

Never before have we seen the level of these vices that we see today. Now, some of these things have always happened, but not to the level we see. Abortion has been part of the problem—legalizing death in the name of convenience. Abortion has replaced slavery as our nation's "original sin", the one that leads to so many other sins. Abortion has contributed to the breakdown of the family, absentee fathers, lack of respect for authority (how can you respect those who advocate death of innocent babies out of convenience).

Unfortunately, I have seen our culture degenerate before our eyes since the sixties. I remember what life was like before this onslaught of evil. I remember the time when most people went to church or at least respected faith. We could talk about it more freely in the public schools, as I did in my high school valedictory address. We have seen the forces of secularism exaggerate the "oppression" of "puritanical values" while replacing them with—nothing but the list of vices Paul warned about above.

---

[60] II Timothy 3:1-5
[61] II Tim. 4:3

We lived without computers and many modern "instant gratifications", but we were happy in large measure. The fifties were a prosperous time in our country when people were proud about "God and country". Was there still a racial problem? Yes. But look at the progress since. Martin Luther King was firmly within the Christian ethic, but look at what's happened recently. Civil rights leaders are no longer talking about equal opportunity, but equal results. Now there are those who would throw away fifty years of progress. There are those who see racism where it doesn't exist. Martin Luther King wanted all to be judged by the "content of their character", not by their socio-economic condition.

Our society has been fragmented into political interest groups instead of being united under the Ten Commandments and the Lord's Prayer.

But we have also thrown away progress by oppressing another whole class of people—the unborn. About the time we began to live up to our creed in one area, we began to take the lives of innocents in another. Where are the civil rights of unborn children? Can we truly say "all lives matter" until the unborn are protected?

Are these the new myths that Paul warned about?[62] A woman's right over her body? The right to take what someone else has because they are more prosperous than you? Myths like "Jesus taught only about love", with no justice or righteousness?

---

[62] II Tim. 4:4

Discipling Insights from the Book of Hebrews

I believe that Paul wrote the Book of Hebrews as his last appeal to the Jews. He did not sign it because he knew that his reputation would preclude those Jews from reading it who needed to hear it. His letters to the Romans and the Hebrews provide a pair of bookends to all his other writings in the New Testament. In Hebrews he takes a very scholarly approach to how the new covenant meshes with the old covenant. I am aware that there are other theories about who wrote Hebrews, but Paul is the one that makes sense to me.

He also gives many final appeals to Jewish disciples of Jesus. Some are warnings. There are definite warnings about not turning back from the faith (Hebrews 6). There are beautiful words about Christ's high priesthood and what he accomplishes in our behalf before the Father. There is the magnificent "hall of faith" in chapter eleven.

There are also practical exhortations in chapters twelve and thirteen that I want to focus on here.

God Disciplines Those He Loves

It's easy to forget that God loves us as a perfect Father. He knows what we need, not just what we want. And so the writer reminds us of this principle:

> *Therefore, since we are surrounded by such a great cloud of witnesses, let us throw off everything that*

hinders and the sin that so easily entangles, and let us run with perseverance the race marked out for us. Let us fix our eyes on Jesus, the author and perfecter of our faith... endure hardship as discipline; God is treating you as sons. For what son is not disciplined by his father? Heb. 12: 1-7 (selected)

Sounds like we'll all have hardships, and God allows them because of his love. Today we call it "tough love" and most parents need more of it for their kids. But in our flesh we wonder why negative things happen and why we don't always have what we want. God is making an eternal investment in us and he wants us to have a "harvest of righteousness and peace", as it points out in verse eleven. This is the way that we share in his holiness.

The writer concludes this chapter by reminding us that "since we are receiving a kingdom that cannot be shaken, let us be thankful, and so worship God acceptably with reverence and awe, for our 'God is a consuming fire'."[63] It is easy to forget what reverence means after a generation of familiarity with God. Yes, he is personal and concerned with each of us. But it is not just <u>about</u> us. The Lord's Prayer reminds us that about seeking His kingdom and His will on earth. We should not take God lightly. There are still times when we should have an attitude of humility in his presence- as when men of God took off their shoes or fell

---

[63] Heb. 12: 28,29

prostrate before him. How many times do we really come before the Lord with this kind of humility?

Sometimes our services are so upbeat that we hesitate to just slow down and spend time before the Lord. We can still do this individually—there is no excuse not to. But we can also learn some things in the corporate gathering before the Lord. Communion provides one opportunity to listen as we spend time in God's presence. But worship can also be designed to lead us into the Holy of Holies and give God time to wash over us. Often this is the time to bring it down to one instrument or voices alone and simply worship and pray a "symphony of prayer".

No matter how we approach worship, people need to be taught to see the value of various types of worship. It doesn't happen by osmosis. We tend to be creatures of habit. In reality, meaningful change in worship is helpful, as long as the people understand the purpose of it. It's not about Preference, but about Purpose. In fact, a very important verse about worship is found in Chapter Thirteen.

Closing Exhortations

There are closing exhortations in Hebrews about purity, marriage and keeping free from the love of money. Regarding worship, Paul says, "let us continually offer to God a sacrifice of praise—the fruit of lips that praise his name."[64] I have said many times

---

[64] Hebrews 13:15

that praise is the fruit of the lips—you have to say it or sing it! Just standing there is not praise (though you can <u>worship</u> without words). There is a reason why God tells us to praise the Lord so many times throughout Scripture. It is for our good, not God's ego. Yet, so many do not actively praise the Lord. Praise is putting our faith into words. God has always emphasized the importance of our words: we overcome by the word of our testimony[65]; with your mouth you confess and are saved[66]; you will have what you say[67] (not for selfish gain, but for God's kingdom).

There are two admonitions in chapter thirteen concerning discipleship. In verse seven we are told to "remember your leaders, who spoke the word of God to you. Consider the outcome of their way of life and imitate their faith." Also, in verse seventeen we are told to "obey your leaders and submit to their authority. They keep watch over you as men who must give an account. Obey them so that their work will be a joy, not a burden, for that would be of no advantage to you." These verses are very relevant to discipleship. Whoever your Paul is, you should remember his words (teaching) and imitate his faith. We are told to obey and submit to the corporate leadership, for they are shepherds watching over you. There is safety in plurality. While we may be discipled by one main person or pastor, it is wise to have a plurality of leadership for balance and safety. Leaders

---

[65] Rev. 12:11
[66] Rom. 10:10
[67] Mark 11:23

should themselves be mutually accountable (pastors to elders and vice versa).

Also in the last few verses is a major clue about who wrote the letter. "I want you to know that our brother Timothy has been released." Now who was it that discipled Timothy?

The Value of a New Members Class

We currently have a new members class that lasts four weeks on Sunday mornings. In the past we have had classes led by the senior pastor that lasted a semester on Wednesday nights. Either way, there are a lot of benefits to these classes. I enjoy teaching the class for several reasons. We cover basics about salvation and church membership. We talk about the unique playbook of our congregation (every congregation has a playbook—the way they normally do things).

But beyond that I continue to meet wonderful new people and potential disciples. We encourage them not only to become members, but to find the blessings of a small group where relationships can grow and they can be discipled further. In our last few classes we have had both young couples, older couples and several singles. We always try to communicate the joy and challenge of knowing God's word. Inevitably, some will respond to the plan of salvation by taking another step toward God, such as baptism. We usually go on a few tangents to answer specific questions that people have. We also have a great opportunity to hear one another's testimonies.

In the past year I have had some great couples in the class. Jeff and Lana came and shared in the class before becoming members. They hope to influence their teenage children for the Lord. Sam and Chrissie came to the class right after becoming members. They are in our praise team and have been a wonderful addition to the church. They recently became small group leaders. Brad and Sarah came to class and learned about the church. She was just baptized a few months ago. Their children are in our wonderful kids program- Kids Quest.

How is Your Faith?

By now we've all heard the phrase "what's in your wallet" a hundred times in a commercial. But let's change the question to "how is your faith?" In preaching a Christmas sermon recently I realized that there were various kinds of faith represented in the story. Zechariah the priest had a **dormant** faith. He and his wife were old and long past child bearing age. In Luke 1 he is in the Holy Place offering incense. It says he has prayed for years for Messiah to come. Yet, his faith was waning. When Gabriel appears to announce that he will be a father to the Forerunner of the Messiah, Zechariah does not believe. For that he is given a lesson he will not soon forget: he is made dumb for the months leading up to the birth of his son. When he arrived home, Elizabeth must have humored him because before long they were expecting a son.

By the time John the Baptist is born, Zechariah's faith was **renewed**. When his tongue was loosed, he poured forth praise and prophesied concerning his son and the Messiah, which he knew was the son in Mary's womb. All of this, of course, strengthened and comforted Mary for the remainder of her pregnancy.

Mary's faith is **active**: she said to Gabriel "be it unto to me as you have said". Later, when Elizabeth confirms that the child in Mary's womb is the Lord, her faith is a **worshiping** faith. She utters the beautiful song of praise known as "The Magnificat".

> *My soul glorifies the Lord and my spirit rejoices in God my Savior, for he has been mindful of the humble state of his servant. From now on all generations will call me blessed, for the Mighty One has done great things for me—holy is his name.*[68]

The praise goes on, but the point here is that she was worshiping, along with Elizabeth. Do you have a worshiping faith? Or is your worship half-hearted and sporadic?

Finally, Joseph and the Magi illustrate the **obedient** faith that we all should have. Joseph obeyed when the Lord reassured him that he should take Mary as his wife. He protected her and then obeyed the dream that told him to flee to Egypt with Mary and baby Jesus. The Magi obeyed by taking a different way home.

---

[68] Luke 1: 46-49

Speaking of Christmas, there are special gifts that God gives unexpectedly. Now this kind of thing doesn't happen all the time to me, but I just received a call, in answer to prayer, from one of our oldest friends in the life of our church. Jack Hacker is 84 years old. He and Joan were some of the first people we met when we came to Fairfield thirty years ago. Jack repaired watches at a local jeweler. He has been in numerous classes I have taught and Joan sang in the choir for all those years until just last year. As their health was declining six months ago, their son took them to live in northern Ohio. It was sudden and understandable, but I missed hearing from Jack. Yesterday I had a fleeting thought that it would be nice to hear from Jack and I tried to think of how I might find his phone number. His old phone had been disconnected.

Suddenly this morning he called! It is the last day of the year and I guess he felt he should contact me. But also, he woke up this morning dreaming about me and the church! That prompted him to call. Sometimes a thought is like a prayer and God hears it!

So we should remember that no matter how long it takes, God answers prayers at unexpected times. Perhaps a house will sell after two years on the market. Perhaps a loved one will recover after months of illness. Someone will call after you were just thinking about them. Or, as I mentioned earlier in the book, someone you discipled or impacted will write you a letter out of the blue after thirty years. Whatever your circumstance, I pray that your faith will be renewed. I pray that your faith will be a worshiping and obedient faith.

Some of us have prayed for years for revival in our land. Some have actively prayed and campaigned against abortion for over forty years. Some have watched the signs and wonder if the return of Christ will be soon. However, after many years, your faith can grow dormant. Just remember that also after many years, the time of fulfillment came when Christ was born two thousand years ago. Once again the time of fulfillment will come when Christians will see their prayers answered and their efforts pay off. Some fulfillments may not happen in the present age, but they will be realized when his Kingdom comes in all its fullness.

Chapter Nine

A Fresh Look at Baptism

Until recently, everyone who named the name of Jesus believed in some form of water baptism. Through history, there have been endless arguments about the timing and method of baptism, but all agreed that it was a necessary part of the initiation of a believer.

Let's look at a few questions and answers about baptism in the Scripture. A lot of times this clears things up for people who may have focused too much on human statements about baptism and not enough on Scripture. It seems a lot better to focus on what baptism is before talking about its relationship to salvation. It is not good to begin by being backed into a corner by some well-intentioned person wanting to know "is it necessary", which I think is the wrong question to begin with.

One of the most obvious questions that baptism answers is "okay, I believe in Jesus Christ, <u>what's next?</u>" This is essentially what happened on the day of Pentecost. The people asked "what shall we do?" Peter answered, *"repent and be baptized in the name of Jesus Christ."* We'll look at the rest of that verse in a moment (Acts 2:38).

Before we go further, we hasten to add that according to many Scriptures, salvation (the new birth) is based on the grace of God and that it is a gift we cannot earn. It is secondly based on faith, our inward response. I like to say that "eternal life begins now for those who believe, according to John 5:24." But who is going to say that the process stops at that point? We must remember that all Scriptures have a context. It is impossible to totally describe salvation or any other concept with one verse of Scripture. We should always look at the entire message and the results (what people did). So please don't think that when I quote one verse, that's all I believe.

In fact, several Scriptures talk about how to put our faith into action- repentance, confession, baptism are among the first things we do. On the day of Pentecost, the Jews realized that the prophet they had killed was, in fact, the Messiah. They were convicted in their hearts. That's faith. There was an internal change, repentance, which caused them to ask what they should do. Peter's reply was a call to action. He said, "Repent and be baptized, every one of you in the name of Jesus Christ for the forgiveness of your sins. And you will receive the gift of the Holy Spirit." Now, everyone knew what baptism was! Some of them had already been baptized for repentance by John the Baptist in the Jordan River. Many had been baptized on their way to worship in the temple, which was called a *mikveh* (immersion bath). There were many places around the temple mount where they could take a baptism. (Many of these places have been excavated on the southern steps of the temple mount in just the last forty years!) The point here is that they were familiar with it, but that Peter was giving it a new meaning.

Now they were to be baptized in the name of Jesus Christ as a part of their forgiveness, or remission of sins. **They realized that Jesus was the ultimate lamb to take away their sins and Peter told them this was a way of identifying with him and thus receiving forgiveness.** They now understood that this was a once for all event. Forgiveness would no longer be based on sacrifices that only lasted a year. Forgiveness was now based upon the death and resurrection of the Messiah (Christ). Perhaps Peter reminded them that Jesus himself had been baptized as an example for us and that he commanded all disciples to be baptized (Matthew 3: 15 and 28: 19-20). But this was not the time to be overly theological, explaining why baptism was their next step. That could come later, after they obeyed the command.

The gift of the Holy Spirit was to be God's gift to people who were believing and obeying the good news. Peter calls this the promise in verse 39, referring to Jesus' promise that the Spirit was coming (as well as many Old Testament prophecies).

In Peter's preaching, we must remember that he was filled and inspired by the Holy Spirit to preach these words and give these instructions. He had just spent three years with Jesus. Jesus had just given the Great Commission a few days earlier and just before his ascension[69] (Matt. 28: 19-20). Though Peter had denied Jesus, Jesus had restored him and Pentecost

---

[69] The commission was given at an appearance in Galilee. The ascension was a few days after later after they had returned to Jerusalem (See Acts 1).

was a fulfillment of what Jesus had said to him about giving him the "keys of the kingdom" back in Matthew 16:19. Peter used the keys here and on other occasions to lead people into the kingdom.

This day is known as the birth of the church. The first time that Jesus' full work was proclaimed and salvation extended in all its fullness. The people responded literally, as evidenced by the fact that 3,000 were baptized that day. "Those who accepted his message were baptized, and about three thousand were added to their number that day." Of course it goes on to say that the people "devoted themselves to the apostles' teaching and to the fellowship, to the breaking of bread and to prayer (2:42).

This seems like a simple, straightforward account, but it has been muddied by years of theological controversy. However, let's stick to the original and proceed. No one can read the gospels and the book of Acts without concluding that <u>the first and literal meaning of baptism is "immersion in water"</u>. For these obedient believers, what had been unholy in their lives was now holy, and they were set apart unto God and made part of the new priesthood of all believers. That they were given a symbolic action to perform in no way detracts from faith and grace. In fact, they had before been filled with guilt and grief at the realization of rejecting Jesus. Now they were cleansed and had a fresh start. They began to practice another symbolic action on a regular basis. The sharing of bread and fruit of the vine in communion represented an ongoing cleansing and fellowship with Jesus, symbolically taking his body and blood.

Putting these two practices together, we have a sign and a meal. Just as Israel had the sign of circumcision and the Passover meal to celebrate their covenant with God, now Christians had their initial sign (baptism) and a meal (communion) to celebrate their new covenant in Christ. Paul compares baptism to circumcision in Colossians 2: 11,12:

> *In him you were also circumcised, in the putting off of the sinful nature, not with a circumcision done by the hands of men but with the circumcision done by Christ, having been buried with him in baptism and raised with him through your faith in the power of God, who raised him from the dead.*

This reminds us that the power of baptism is faith in Jesus and his resurrection. With this understanding we are set free from our sinful nature.[70] This is one of the two places where Paul refers to immersion in water as a burial. And regarding our covenant meal, remember Jesus had said, "do this in remembrance of me". The message never was "you don't need the physical, just the spiritual". That violates the principle of literal interpretation.

---

[70] See Herbert M. Carson, *The Epistles of Paul to the Colossians and Philemon,* Tyndale New Testament Commentaries, Pg.67.

Acts 10

Another question arises in Acts 10 as Peter visits the household of Cornelius, the first Gentile convert. In this case the question is raised by Peter. Remember that the early Jewish believers were hesitant to reach out the Gentiles with the Gospel, or perhaps were just waiting for God's instructions how to do it. Through a vision and a dream, God had appeared to both Cornelius to send for Peter, and to Peter to go with the Gentile messengers. Peter arrives and proclaims the work of Jesus. It's a beautiful sermon and during his preaching the Holy Spirit falls on the household. "The circumcised believers who had come with Peter were astonished that the gift of the Holy Spirit had been poured out even on the Gentiles. For they heard them speaking in tongues and praising God." This has often been called the Pentecost for the Gentiles. There was no doubt that God had accepted them!

Now Peter asks a rhetorical question; "<u>Can anyone keep these people from being baptized with water?</u> They have received the Holy Spirit just as we have. So he ordered that they be baptized in the name of Jesus Christ." (Acts 10: 45-48) He was careful not to stop short of the goal of the Great Commission. So they were baptized in water, as well as in the Spirit. I believe this is the intention for every believer. Again, it's not an either/or thing, although tongues is certainly not the only evidence of the Spirit. The attempt by some to spiritualize baptism ignores the principles of literalness and context.

Paul's Preaching

There were three incidents recorded regarding Paul and questions and answers about baptism. These references are likewise from the Book of Acts. One was with the Philippian jailer in Acts 16, one with the Ephesian disciples in Acts 19 and one as he shares his testimony in Acts 22.

After a dramatic story of Paul and Silas in prison, an earthquake and the near suicide of the jailer, a question is asked by the jailer. "<u>What must I do to be saved?</u>" Paul and Silas's answer, and the first thing we should say is, "Believe in the Lord Jesus, and you will be saved—you and your household." (vs. 31). But we must let the entire story speak. Whatever your feeling about baptism, Paul did not neglect it. Here's the "rest of the story". "Then they spoke the word of the Lord to him and to all the others in his house. At that hour of the night the jailer took them and washed their wounds; then immediately he and all his family were baptized." So there was a time of teaching, but not long. Once the jailer heard more details, he did not hesitate on baptism. (KJV says that same hour of the night...) How poignant that the jailer cleansed their wounds and then was cleansed of his sins!

By the way, we assume that all those of the household were believers when they were baptized, otherwise they would not have fulfilled Paul's initial command to believe. This would eliminate children too young to believe and so is not an example of infant baptism.

Another instance is Paul's conversation with the Ephesian disciples in Acts 19. They apparently believed in Jesus but had only heard of the baptism of John. They had not heard of the fullness of baptism in the name of Jesus and for the Holy Spirit.

> *Paul asked them, "Did you receive the Holy Spirit when you believed?"*
>
> *They answered, "No, we have not even heard that there is a Holy Spirit."*
>
> *So Paul asked, "Then what baptism did you receive?"*
>
> *"John's baptism," they replied.*
>
> *Paul said, "John's baptism was a baptism of repentance. He told the people to believe in the one coming after him, that is, in Jesus." On hearing this, they were baptized into the name of the Lord Jesus. Acts 19:2-5*

Paul's questions here reveal that he sensed something was missing in these disciples- the Holy Spirit. When he realized that they did not have all the facts, he filled them in and they were baptized correctly. This is a good example for us of how to proceed with someone is partially taught. When they were obedient (and after Paul laid his hands on them), they received the

Holy Spirit, reminding us of Peter's statement in Acts 5:32 that God gives the Spirit to those who obey him.

Some today do not seem to like the idea that baptism represents cleansing and forgiveness. They seem to be missing a great blessing. Doesn't it make sense that God has given us a simple action that we will always remember to associate with our time of accepting Jesus? Do they want to ignore the beautiful feelings that most people experience when they go in and out of the water in Jesus' name? <u>Why minimize something God has given us?</u>

Paul had no such qualms. When telling his testimony to the Jews in Acts 22:16 he recounts his conversion experience. This time Ananias asks the question:

> *Then he (Ananias) said, "The God of our fathers has chosen you to know his will and to see the Righteous One and to hear words from his mouth. You will be his witness to all men of what you have seen and heard. <u>And now what are you waiting for?</u> Get up, be baptized and wash your sins away, calling on his name."*

What are you waiting for? That's a question we need to ask. Paul associated his baptism with the washing away of sins. Paul felt no need to analyze this, he simply tells it as part of the story. And the implication is that he did not hesitate. We can see from these three passages that whether he was talking with Philippian Gentiles, or Ephesian disciples, or Jerusalem Jews, the message was always the same.

The above passages and precedents should be sufficient for our obedience in baptism. But we can certainly draw additional conclusions about why it is important from other passages:

It's a definite action at a point of time.

It's a physical act for physical beings.

It's a symbol of cleansing and a celebration of forgiveness.

It has value as a public proclamation to witnesses.

It is an act of good conscience, as Peter says later in I Peter 3:21.

It's a reference to Jesus' death and resurrection (Rom. 6:3 and Col. 2:12)

It's compared to the sign of circumcision in Col. 2:12.

These are not small or insignificant reasons. Let us neither give more, nor less emphasis to this blessed event than the Scriptures do. Let us respond joyfully to the opportunity to follow Christ in baptism. Let's share the Scriptures and let people decide. Don't let someone back you into a corner with unproductive questions like "Do I have to be baptized?" Or "can I be saved without being baptized?" "Or what if someone dies on the way to be baptized?" Giving a simplistic answer without Scripture will lead to argument and lead people to believe you are saved by baptism alone, even if you don't believe that. And they will take your answer as opinion even if it is Scriptural. Instead, ask them if they will look at the Scriptures with you and let the Holy Spirit convict them.

History= His story

I like that phrase and I like the fact that there are so many faith stories through history. Now some people don't get in to history, but I love it. It inspires me. It is also important to see how God has worked in every century in amazing ways. I wanted to first give you the previous faith stories from our church and my life to show that God is working right here in our midst. But we certainly should not neglect the great conversions and movements through history. So here is a list of major ways how God has moved and brought lessons to us all through the history of the church. If you have further interest in any one of these areas, you can google it!

Most of us know that most of these people and movements were not perfect. Yet, God uses those who are willing and available to accomplish great things.

Things and People God Has Used to Bring Salvation

God used The Nation of Israel to bring Christ (the Messiah) into the world.

God used The Greek Language to spread the good news and the New Testament.

God used Roman Roads as the pathways for preachers.

God used The Church Fathers to affirm true doctrines for 300 years:

They witnessed to the authentic Scriptures.

God used the Martyrs to witness to faith stronger than death!

God used The Monasteries and the Scribes to accurately transmit the Scriptures during the Middle Ages.

God used The Missionaries to reach the nations.

God used The Separatists to convict the church of sin and corruption;

Hussites, Waldensians, Anabaptists and others.

God used The Printing Press to prepare the way for Reformation- 1450's on:

The Bible in the languages and hands of the people;

Wycliffe and Tyndale English translations led to The King James Version;

Translations in the languages of the people.

God used The Reformation and men like Luther, Calvin and Zwingli to reform the Church (the beginning of a process)- 1500's; *sola Scriptura, sola fide (faith).*

God used The Kings of Spain and England to spread Christianity to the New World;

From King Henry to King James- 1600's

This led to the migration of Pilgrims and Puritans.

God used Christianity to bring universal education in the U.S.

God used The American Revolution to spearhead the separation of church and state (no state church).

God used our Judeo-Christian foundation to bring forth documents such as the Declaration of Independence and The Constitution.

God used The First Great Awakening to prepare the nation for the Revolution;

John Wesley and George Whitefield

God used the Restoration Movement to challenge denominationalism- 1800's;

I Cor. 1: 10-13, Eph. 4:3-6. Barton Stone and Alexander Campbell were leaders.

God used The Second Great Awakening to prepare the nation for the Civil War.

God used Abolitionist preachers to raise the banner against slavery.

God used Revivalism to challenge dead orthodoxy and higher criticism- II Tim. 3:16, Heb. 4:12. Finney, Moody and Billy Sunday were outstanding.

God used Pentecostalism to challenge Rationalism- 1900's; I Cor. 1:18-25, 2:1-10.

God used the rebirth of Israel to challenge Replacement Theology- 1948- Isaiah 11:11-12, Ezekiel 37, Romans 11: 25-28.

God used the Dead Sea Scrolls to challenge religious liberalism- Isaiah 66:8- 1948 to the present.

God used Scientific Creationism to challenge evolution- 1960's to present; II Peter 3:3-7. Creation Research Institute and Answers in Genesis among others.

At the same time, God used the Charismatic Movement to cut across many denominational lines and renew a balanced emphasis on the Holy Spirit.

God used the Jesus Movement (with its contemporary music) and Prophecy Movement to attract young people and to challenge a rigid church culture- 1970's. Psalm 150 was once again applied and Christian music festivals became common. God has used many musicians and groups to cross racial barriers for the last fifty years.

God used Campus ministries to challenge secular humanism- I Peter 3:15; Navigators, Campus Crusade for Christ, Inter Varsity

God used Evangelists and television to win souls for the kingdom- Billy Graham and many others- Romans 1:16. Don't let the few failures distract from the many faithful!

God used the Worship Movement of the last thirty years to bring unity- Romans 15: 5-9. Media companies like Maranatha and Integrity Music have spread worship music and products. Christian record companies have contributed.

God used the Messianic Movement to restore the awareness of Jewish roots of Christianity and witness to Jews around the world; Jews for Jesus, Chosen People Ministries, Jewish Voice Ministries

God used the Modern Missions Movement to spread the faith to millions around the world, including the work of Bible translation into hundreds of tribal languages.

Christian Apologists

There have been outstanding Christian writers in every age that have witnessed to the truth of Christianity and its various lines of evidence (called apologetics). I hope you have one or two favorites. These writers use historical, archaeological and documental evidence to reinforce foundations of our faith. Some of the arguments, like fulfilled prophecy, go back to the New Testament (Paul) and the church fathers of the early centuries. Other lines of evidence are more recent.

C.S. Lewis, author of *Mere Christianity,* influenced his generation during World War II and after. (He died on the same day as John F. Kennedy.) F.F. Bruce is another excellent British apologist and professor, and expert on the New Testament documents.

Josh McDowell, Lee Strobel[71], David Limbaugh[72], and Ravi Zacharias are some of my favorites from recent years. I encourage you to pick an area of interest in apologetics and read what these men have to say. They support the historicity of Jesus and the New Testament documents (and the Old as well). They show how archaeology has a role, despite its many gaps, in corroborating Scripture. They repeat effective philosophical arguments, evidence for the resurrection, etc. Two of them are lawyers by training.

While we're on this topic, we should share a great resource for the correct understanding of Islam. This is one of the most crucial and misunderstood issues of our time. There are many who have written comparative religion books with sections on Islam. But the best resource is a book called *Unveiling Islam* by Ergun and Emir Caner. The Caner brothers grew up in Gahanna, Ohio. They are from a Muslim, Turkish background. Their father built one of the first

---

[71] *The Case for Christ and the Case for Faith*
[72] *Jesus on Trial*

mosques in Columbus. As teens they accepted Jesus and have become professors of theology in universities. Their book came out in 2002, but has been pretty much ignored by the secular world. They expose many of the politically correct myths we have been hearing for several years. They are respectful, but realistic regarding Islam and the root causes of its violence. False hopes and untruths help no one.

Another recent book that has been inspiring and comprehensive in its coverage of apologetics is *The Politically Incorrect Guide to the Bible* by Robert Hutchinson.

Once again I can say that, thanks to these resources, I have not heard any arguments from skeptics and critics over the last decades that have carried much weight. There are answers to each one of them if you look.

Chapter Ten

Blessings Over the Years

Many of my blessings have already been chronicled in these pages. They are the people with whom I have worked and invested. It is a joy to see them serving. But there are also blessings over the years of being part of a team that has built the church and enabled us to host many wonderful guests over the years.

My first thirteen years here we worked hard to build a congregation of 1200 and built the worship center in 1998. At that time we still had a relatively small staff. Little did I realize how many opportunities that worship center would provide over the next seventeen years. While I had little to do with our Christian school, I have been gratified to see how our efforts have touched the lives of hundreds of students by providing a facility for them, and for many of the teachers who have come from our congregation.

In more recent years the church has provided opportunities for me to direct choirs and ensembles at Christmas and other times, with a wonderful stage and sound system. There have been many opportunities to lead the worship team, sing solos and duets in Easter productions, sing in a Pastors Trio, preach, and do special praise gatherings. (I've already mentioned the blessing of producing our original Easter production.)

The church has hosted many Gospel concerts, speakers like Tim LaHaye, Ken Ham and Josh McDowell (hosted by the school); sports star speakers, particularly at school events that even included the OSU Alumni Band (which I have participated in over the years)! I never thought I would be playing with them on <u>our</u> stage!

We've hosted many missionaries over the years from all parts of the world. While they may not be on the Who's Who list in our society, they certainly are in the Kingdom of God! Many have labored faithfully over the years in difficult fields of ministry and we like to hear from them when they are in town. Talk about inspiring our local disciples to do more!

We've hosted contemporary music and arts groups like Ballet Magnificat, Avalon, Anointed, Twila Paris, Stephen Curtis Chapman, the Glory Revealed Tour, Maranatha Worship Seminars, Newsong and many others. We've hosted countless Gospel Music concerts. We've hosted orchestras like the Lancaster Festival Orchestra, Fairfield Christian Academy school musicals and orchestras like "Fiddler on the Roof" and "Meet Me in St. Louis". We've done two Christmas productions recently including "Scrooge" with sound tracks and "The Journey" with live orchestra.

We've had many in-house praise gatherings with our various worship leaders and teams and our own dance ministry. In addition, our resident dance teacher has had many recitals in our wonderful facility. God has been good. We are excited about a <u>new</u> season of praise and prayer gatherings! This is such an important part of ministry as we move ahead. Nothing lasting happens without prayer. Jesus said that "if we abide in him" we will bear much fruit. It is my privilege to work with a wonderful team of prayer ministry people.

Another track that has developed is our support of messianic ministries like Jews for Jesus and Chosen People Ministries. I remember the first time David Brickner came and did "Christ in the Passover" in our old chapel. That was before he became executive director of Jews for Jesus. Since then he has been back several times and spoken in our worship center. Other missionaries from that organization and Chosen People Ministry have graced our stage. Perhaps we have been a small encouragement to these ministries that reach around the world.

Another highlight was the year we had Israeli guests and Paul Wilbur here together. The Israelis were from the Israel Leadership Institute, sponsored by Alliance for the Future of Israel[73]. They were not messianic, but one of them was a paratrooper in 1967 when Israel took back Old Jerusalem and the Wailing Wall. His name was General Oded Tyrah. Now <u>there</u> was a person of history right on our stage! These folks heard the gospel several times that weekend, both from Paul's music and from our pastor Ken Mulpas.

My prayer is that these events have raised awareness of prophecy, Israel and God's work in the world today. If you have been a disciple in the life of our

---

[73] Susan Lhota

church, you will remember many of these events. If you are new in the life of the church, it is an example of the many things God can do through a faithful church and faithful disciples such as yourself. Satan wants you to feel like a drop in the bucket, but God says you are a "living stone built into a spiritual house to be a holy priesthood".[74] Don't underestimate what God can do through faithful servants working together in a healthy church! No, it's not a perfect church, but we have enjoyed many years of health and ministry.

My prayer for our church is that we will let God make us the church he wants us to be. Let us be the pastors and people he wants us to be. While we have had blessings in the past, it is more important that we look to the future. As Paul said in Philippians and is always relevant:

> *Forgetting what is behind and straining toward what is ahead, I press on toward the goal to win the prize for which God has called me heavenward in Christ Jesus.*[75]

We should not live in either the pain or the glory of the past, but look for the glory of the future! There are seasons of diligent labor, and then seasons of harvest. So let us plant seeds in the hearts of people and cultivate their growth for the harvest that is to come! I pray for people that will not run down the street, always seeking some new experience without

---

[74] I Peter 2:5
[75] Philippians 3:13

putting forth the tilling and cultivation of the soil where they are planted. Lord, give us patience that in due time we will reap a harvest. We can get lost in the moment, but let us never quit looking for the goal and the prize.

Wedding Blessings

Weddings are a holy season and moment in time to share with couples. I have been blessed to do counseling and weddings for a number of couples over the years. Many were in the life of our church, or relatives of members. Some have stayed active in our church for many years and raised their children here.

Two of my favorites were the Shreyer twins. Amanda, and then Alyson, asked me to do their weddings. Their parents, Tom and Roberta have been our friends for over fifteen years. In the last few years I have been honored to perform weddings for nieces, nephews and cousins. In addition to church weddings, many have taken place in parks, lodges, and even the ninth hole of a golf course. (Make that two golf courses since I just returned from officiating a cousin's wedding in Phoenix.)

Colleagues and Elders

I have mentioned many of the men who served as pastors and shepherds here over the years. I am grateful to them for their contributions to the church and to my life. Outstanding leaders such as Ken Mulpas have served over a long period, including years as Executive and Senior Pastor. He has served this congregation nearly twenty years. We have had some great pastoral teams and once again we have a great one. I look forward to serving with Dean Woodward, our new Senior Pastor, over the next few years.

Besides several of the men mentioned above, there have been many long serving elders like Charlie Black and Jim Morris that have helped us through storms and been supportive of me.[76] Doug Cronin, Glen Starner and Doug Ramey have been supportive elders in recent times.

There are other friends and faith stories along the way that I have not included, but are equally significant and precious to us. There are too many people to thank for their encouragement along the way.

We are excited about our new youth minister, Scott Stem. He brings energy and enthusiasm to our teen youth program and is already investing in the lives of young people here.

Donna's Healing

The last testimony in this book is the one I just received from a sister who has been reaching out to and discipling others, including Diana who was mentioned earlier in these pages.

---

[76] Other friends who now serve in other ministries deserve a shout out: Mark Howes, Norm Anderson, Matt Dilger, Tom Lacey, Mark Bunton, Mark Zeltman, Mike and Tom Milby, Randy Benedetto and Bill McWhorter.

Donna Roark's heart was attacked by a virus in 2012. She had Myocarditis. She became ill and disoriented very quickly and ended up in ICU. The next day my wife and I saw her there nearly unconscious, but barely able to acknowledge my presence. I prayed, but knew she was critically ill. Here is the story in her own words:

"While in ER I kept fading in and out, my heart was only pumping at 15%. They had a hard time diagnosing me because of my history of COPD. I was admitted to ICU, intubated and put on a heart pump along with antibiotics. My husband asked if I was going to live and was told they didn't know. Three days would tell the tale... My family, my church family and many from other churches were praying for me. Thank God for prayer warriors: without them I would not be here today...

"My doctors could not believe how quickly I recovered. I was moved to a regular room after three days in ICU. Then after being in the hospital for nine days I came home. At first I was nervous to be in my bedroom again, but I kept telling myself 'it's okay because God healed me!' God the Father, Creator of the Universe had healed me!

"During that time I was aware of spiritual warfare around me—it seemed that demons were trying to stop the prayers. Though it was very intense I was not afraid. Two weeks later the doctor told me to stop taking the medication and that he would not need to see me again. That was several years ago and I have not had any heart issues since!

> *"I will never forget the love and compassion from my family, Fairfield Christian Church, River Valley Life Center (and two other churches). Thank you all. Most of all, thank you Jesus."*

Yes, God is still at work and whether we realize it or not, we need Him and our Christian family!

Open the Eyes of My Heart, Lord[77]

All of us are challenged at times by change. Many of us can be suspicious of motives of others, especially when their methods are different from our norm. **Learning to look beneath the surface is a desirable trait for disciples.** The church over the last forty years has developed and changed in a lot of surface ways. Sometimes we employ new tools to help people learn or worship. But the Message is the same. One thing to remember is that we are all different. Our responses can be very different to the same stimuli.

There is still the power and influence of the preaching pastor. People often judge churches on the style of the pastor. Many churches have added dynamic music programs, worship and youth pastors, or corporate looking megachurch characteristics. All of these additions offer much good and none are perfect. I believe the great majority of them are sincere.

---

[77] Song by Paul Baloche

But we must not lose sight of simple truths: for example, the value of a pastor that sincerely presents Christ and a portion of His word. We should look beyond style to the heart. Copying a style has its limitations. We should each be the pastor God has created us to be.

Worship still needs to be "in Spirit and in truth", whether it is led by one voice, a choir, a piano, guitar or band. I have experienced true worship in all these formats. Again, we should look beyond the instruments and styles to the hearts of the leaders. Whatever the music type, I love all these "vehicles" that help us express praise and worship to the King, especially when they are presented skillfully (Psalm 33:3).

I have also learned that every culture contributes to the kingdom of God. When the word says, "let all the peoples praise him", I believe that means all cultures. Many of us grow up with one or two styles (or cultures) of worship. All the families of nations are to "ascribe to the Lord glory and strength", according to Ps. 96:7. Do all the tribes do that the same way? Of course not.

I grew up in the praise of a white, European middle class culture. Fortunately, I had friends of other cultures close by. I will never forget the first African American church revival I attended while in college. The people helped the preacher all through his message! (The most I had heard before was an occasional "Amen".) The singing style was different and truly from the "soul". I have always appreciated the joy and expression behind that style: however different it seemed, these folks were still praising God from their hearts.

So whether it is a white choir in the Midwest, a multicultural choir like the Brooklyn Tabernacle Choir, or the black choirs of Atlanta or Los Angeles, I can enjoy the worship. Later I learned to appreciate the Hebrew style of worship found among many messianic believers today. Whether it is worship led from a piano, or a guitar, I can enjoy it. Whether it is loud or soft, I can enjoy it. Whether a flute or trumpet or cello or violin is added, I can enjoy it.

Our church culture has come a long way. We were very homogenous thirty years ago. But change was inevitable. I remember about 25 years ago a lady objecting to a tambourine used with some up tempo songs in our worship. She said "I'd like to throw that thing in the trash." Was she reflecting some bad experience or association? Was she afraid of losing a tradition she was used to? At any rate, I reminded that that was only less than five minutes of the worship service! She was letting that little segment upset her for the rest of the time! Guess what. She made it over the hump and finished her life worshiping with us. But the truth is, we all have some stumbling blocks that shift our focus away from God's intent: the music is too loud, too soft; not enough hymns, not enough verses...and on and on.

In this regard, I like the 11th Commandment: **Blessed are the flexible, for they shall not be fractured.** The answer is to look for the Lord, not your preference. Avoid the consumer mentality. Once in a while you can experience your preference, but don't look for it too often—there are a hundred or thousand other folks with their own preferences too!! No worship leader or pastor can cover them all. Variety is still the spice of life and of worship. Don't sit there wishing for what you had last week, last month, or last year. Look for what the Lord is saying to you <u>now</u> on a regular basis. He is speaking! Are you listening?

Or is your mind too cluttered with preferences or criticisms? Do you wish the sermon was more topical? Or more expository? Do you wish there were more illustrations? The person next to you might be wishing for fewer illustrations and more "meat".

Yet even the best preacher, orchestra, choir or band in the world can sometimes miss God. That's where we need His grace. Pray for them. After all, you missed God today also! Or if you haven't yet, you need to get out of bed!

Have you ever heard people from the same event say opposite things? I have! "I wish the speaker was louder." "I wish he would pipe down." "I wish that lady hadn't hit the high note." "My spine just tingled when she hit that high note." It was too hot or too cold. The worship was too long, or "I was just getting into it when it stopped." Communion should be before the message. Communion should be after the message.

There are endless opinions because there are an endless variety of people. But consider the opposite. A congregation or service where everything is predictable is boring. Imagine if they actually did the same song or set every week!

Services are often a balancing act between various options. How about balancing spontaneity with "decent and in order"? "Making a joyful noise" versus "blending in"? The lights are too bright, the lights are too low. We've heard it all. Some say, "the low lights help me worship" while others say, "the low lights make it too much like a performance." And that was the same service!

If you try, you can always find something good about a service. Conversely, if you try, you can always find something not so good. Which mood are you in? To which voice will you listen? Do you want your leaders to be God centered, or people paranoid? Many people are used to finding their favorite spots to sit at secular events, but will not look for their sweet spot at church. They don't expect the secular world to revolve around them, yet they will expect that of the church. Attitude will always determine your altitude. Remember you have a spiritual enemy who wants to distract you from God's Spirit and what He wants to do in you- in Spirit and in truth!

Grace and Significance

By the grace of God I am what I am." I Cor. 15:10

In both our giftings and our role, we are what we are by God's grace. Paul called himself the least of the apostles and some looked down on him because he was not part of the original Twelve. That is ironic, since many today consider him to be the greatest apostle. But he knew it was all by God's grace— grace that saved him from a life of works righteousness in Judaism; that turned him from persecutor to defender of the faith; that overcame his sense of unworthiness and the unfavorable comparisons many made of him.

Today, I am what I am by God's grace—an all-purpose pastor who has been graciously called to serve this church for thirty years. Hard to believe! I helped in the building years; I have tried to be a stabilizing factor in the lean years and the years the "locusts" of debt have eaten.[78] God has given me the opportunity of shepherding and discipling hundreds of people. Many have gone on to other ministries and are still serving the Lord. Maybe I made some positive contributions to their faith and worship. I have trained a dozen teachers and encouraged others.

God has called me to stand for his Word, for worship and for the salvation that comes through Christ alone. I have also tried to stand for less typical positions in areas such as the work of the Holy Spirit, the role of

---

[78] Joel 2: 25 promises to restore the years the locusts have eaten.

Israel in God's plan, and the freedom to express worship in various ways including the arts. In these areas I have tried to see beyond the traditional (and sometimes unexamined) positions of my background. My wife says I have often "taken the road less traveled". I am grateful for other pastors and teachers in the body of Christ that have led me in my journey of discipleship and discovery.

Though at times I have wondered if all my gifts were being used, the fact is that they have been, in due season. Despite the fact that I have not had a title that some would consider most important, I have had influence. I have been privileged to be part of a leadership team, which I think is the ideal anyway. Titles are overrated. They also make one a target, both for adulation and criticism. They may lead people to believe that you have answers that only God has— for example the survival and future of the church. That is ultimately God's grace rather than man's effort.

I am only pointing out some of these things to illustrate the different ways that God works in each of us. Don't underestimate what He can do and the things only you can do in a given situation. Don't discount your uniqueness!

To be able to preach often in the interim year of 2009 was significant (and a few times each year since). To lead worship a dozen times a year for about four of those transition years was also significant and helped provide stability for our people during the transition to our present worship pastor. To baptize many and lead them to church membership over the years has been a joy for me. Even leading twelve to eighteen funerals a year has been an opportunity to minister to many families.

My occasional teachings and sermons on prophecy have encouraged others. Our former police chief happened to be visiting during one of those sermons and reminds me about it when I see him.

Many have appreciated my books and articles over the years, even though the books were self-published and limited in distribution. To God be the glory! I thank God for the wonderful people in the life of our church who have supported and encouraged my ministry over the years. These thirty years would not have been possible without them. Some have given me books and ideas at just the right time to stimulate my creativity. And I am grateful for their prayers through the years. Special thanks to my calling partner, Jerry Bender, who has encouraged my book projects over the years.

Also, special thanks to my friends, Les and Tracy King who helped in the publishing of this book.

So whatever you do for the kingdom, may you not become "weary in doing good, for in due time you will reap a harvest if you do not give up."[79] I dedicate this book to my grandchildren: Aaron and Evan Sines;

---

[79] Gal. 6:9

Abbie, Michael and Claire Whitcraft. Though you are young now, maybe someday you'll read Papa's stories.

And to the reader, thank you for reading these stories of discipleship. May God bless you with your own stories to tell!

Postlude

The Testimonies in Alphabetical Order

Shawn Banker

Stacie Blankenship

J.T. and Karen Burcham

John and Ardella Campbell

Dale and Marian Curtis

Steve Elkins

Greg and Jeanette Elliott

Sean and Rachel Frazier

Joe and Trish Gormley

Dale and Kim Harris

Bill and Margaret Hines

Diana Lax

Joe and Erin Morris

Jason Morris

Phil and Megan Peters

Dave and Loretta Phalen

Marc and Tina Phillips

Tom and Toby Rapp

Joel Reid

Donna Roark

Rocky and Penni Robbins

Pat Schindler

Jack and Becky Schumacher

Joel Seymour

Robin Sigler

Dan Spires

Glen and Carol Starner

Nancy Stevens

Jay and Terri Stump

Ron and Donna Weisenberger

May the Postlude continue to play with many future testimonies of discipleship!

About the Author

Mark just celebrated his fortieth year in ministry. He grew up in Columbus, Ohio and received his bachelor' degree from The Ohio State University. He completed his Master's Degree at the Cincinnati Bible Seminary. Since 1985 he has been a pastor at the Fairfield Christian Church in Lancaster, Ohio.

His other books include a series of historical fiction works on the gospels. This was followed by a study of the book of Acts and the church of today. More recently he wrote *A 21st Century Look at the Old Testament.*

In addition to his pastoral responsibilities and work as Discipleship Pastor, he has also been a worship leader and speaker.

He resides with his wife Lori in Lancaster. They have three children and five grandchildren. He enjoys travel, music, and golf.

Made in the USA
Middletown, DE
02 October 2016